KONAPEE'S EDEN

Historic and Scenic Handbook

The Columbia River Gorge

by

Oral Bullard

TMS Book Service
Box 1504
Beaverton, OR 97075

I.S.B.N. 911518-69-X

For Suzanne
soul and help-mate
extraordinaire

Area Map

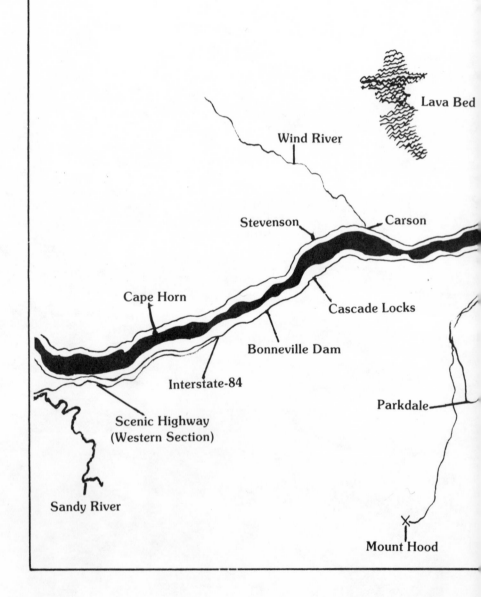

Lava Bed

Wind River

Stevenson

Carson

Cape Horn

Cascade Locks

Bonneville Dam

Interstate-84

Scenic Highway
(Western Section)

Parkdale

Sandy River

Mount Hood

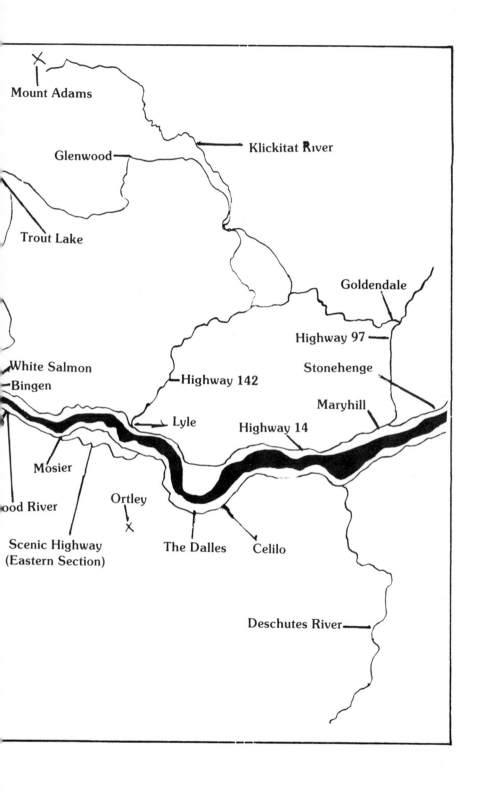

Mount Adams

Klickitat River

Glenwood

Trout Lake

Goldendale

Highway 97

White Salmon

Bingen

Highway 142

Stonehenge

Maryhill

Lyle

Highway 14

Mosier

Ortley

od River

Scenic Highway
(Eastern Section)

The Dalles

Celilo

Deschutes River

Contents

In the beginning . . .

It was born of violence, then shaped by convulsive eruptions and catastrophic floods.

Today we marvel at the idyllic beauty of the Gorge of the Columbia, that 90-mile channel which conveys America's fourth largest river through the Cascade Range. Viewed at any point along the way, from the barren desert at its eastern end to the lush forests at the western terminus, the Gorge offers a tranquil scene of surpassing beauty. It is difficult to imagine it in any other form.

But 40 million years ago the earth crust of Western America was buckled by massive pressures. It writhed and heaved, was rent by great fissures from which poured streams of molten lava. The sky was filled with smoke and ash, the darkness lit by fiery volcanoes which rose to form the peaks of the Cascade Range.

Millions of years later, after these upheavals were stilled, glacier ice sheets pushed down from the north to cover more than one-fourth the surface of the earth. It was only 20,000 years ago that these ice sheets retreated. In that process they left a 2,000 foot ice and debris dam behind which a gigantic lake extended for hundreds of miles into the valleys of western Montana.

When this dam was breached an estimated 400 cubic miles of water, equal to 40 percent of today's Lake Michigan, was released in a matter of less than 2 weeks. This incredible flood scoured the eastern Washington plateau, creating coulees and dry falls still evident, before forming another lake (Condon) beyond Crown point. When the water poured out of that second lake it put the Willamettte Valley under 400 feet of water as far south as Eugene.

This mammoth flood, reminiscent of some descriptions of Biblical fury, is said to have repeated itself as many as 40 times over a period of 7,000 years.

In time the scarred land healed. Grass carpeted the slopes, trees grew, flowers blossomed. Animals came to graze and birds built nests in the trees and sang their songs in counterpoint to the melody of the rushing water of the Columbia.

Then, most probably via a land bridge from Asia, the first human settlers arrived. They viewed the bounty of the great river, settled along its banks

7

and formed a civilization an estimated 10,000 or more years ago.

One theory has it that the western continents were populated by migration from this point. Others disagree. No matter. One thing is certain, over the centuries Celilo Falls became the great gathering place for the Indians of Western America. Here they established what has been called "the trading mart of the Columbia." Each summer they came from far places, the Rocky Mountains, the southwest, from Minnesota and the plains.

These travelers brought with them goods that were native to their part of the country and engaged in trade with the coastal and river tribes for such things as dried oysters and clams, for sea fish, berries and roots. The local Indians also marketed wapato, a root bulb which grew in the western lowlands and which was harvested by women who hung their legs over the sides of canoes and scooped the root from underwater with their toes. They dried salmon by exposing the fish to the sun on scaffolds erected along the river bank. When the fish was sufficiently dry it was pounded into powder between stones, pressed and packed in bales of grass matting about two feet long by one foot in diameter, lined with cured salmon skins. The top of each bale was likewise covered with skins and secured with a cord, then twelve of these bales, seven on the bottom row, five on the top row, were formed into a package containing between ninety and one hundred pounds of dried salmon which would keep for several years. A few pinches of the fish meal was sufficient to flavor soup or other dishes and it was in great demand.

The fishermen at Celilo and the Long Narrows—that section of the Columbia below the falls where it was said "the river turned sideways" as it rushed through a narrow chasm—were the middlemen in the trading and bartering that went on.

A number of tribes, or families, of Indians lived along the river and they were lumped together under the name Chinook. Those living at Celilo were called the Eneechurs and they got along well with other upriver families, while those at the Narrows were named Escheloots. They had strong ties with tribes downriver.

Any animosities between these various families were largely forgotten when the annual pilgrimage to Celilo occurred. This was more than a gathering place. It was a fair, a convention. It was also called "the Monte Carlo of the aboriginies" for the Indians were basically fun loving gamblers who enjoyed races and various games of chance.

This civilization existed for thousands of years before the intrusion of the white race. Many of the artifacts which might reveal more of that period's history are buried now beneath the water impounded by the dams which stilled the wild rush of the Columbia during the mid-Twentieth century.

So what lives on from those days is a series of legends. Told and retold throughout these many years, with probably some exaggeration or variation in the re-telling, they remain as the record we now possess of those ancient times.

In this respect Indian lore seems to be at least as accurate as the early white man's tales, many of which we now know to have been outright falsehoods.

But there are those legends and tales, from both Indian and white sources, which can be neither proved nor disproved. These hint at things which may have been different than recorded history reveals. In that difference there is both mystery and romance, which is, after all, the stuff of which legends are made.

Legends, early discovery tales, folklore and adventures . . .

He was 75-years old and nearly blind when Lewis and Clark met him at Celilo Falls on their trip home in 1806. His name, he said, was Soto and he was the son of the Spaniard, Konapee, who had been shipwrecked on the coast near the mouth of the great river. From there Konapee had migrated upstream to this place, the crossroads of the Western Indian world, where he became a man of importance, one of the chiefs of the Indian tribes.

Fact, fantasy or fable?

Lewis and Clark arrived in the Northwest 13 years after Robert Gray sailed his ship across the bar in May, 1792, and a week later named the river Columbia, after the vessel which had made the first entry into the Great River of the West.

History records discoveries which are duly reported through proper channels and written down. Only when they are thus documented are they recognized, officially. Thus, although there is evidence that other ships and persons from the Western civilization had entered the river prior to Gray's dramatic trip across the Columbia bar these visits are relegated to the background, treated as folklore because of lack of documentation.

Three hundred years earlier Christopher Columbus became the "official" discoverer of a new world, although it is now believed that others— particularly the Vikings and probably some Africans as well—had beaten him to the Americas shores by decades or even centuries.

Many of the early adventurers wrote no history at all. In some cases, what they did write was to fit their needs, to impress whoever was backing them and thus ensure financing for another voyage of discovery. Because so much was unknown it was easy to report on or theorize about geographical features which might not even exist.

Consider Gaspar Cortereall, a Portugese navigator who may have set in motion one of the greatest hunts in history, the almost 3 century long search for the Straits of Anian.

Only 8 years after Columbus made his famous voyage Cortereall explored along the North American Coast between Labrador and the Bay of Fundy. He did not return from his last voyage, begun in 1501, and when his brother Miguel set out to find him in 1502 he also failed to make it home.

So Gaspar Cortereall's moment in history is short-lived and rates only a minor note except for the fact it is believed he was the first to suggest the existence of a navigable passage across the newly found continent. No matter that the distance across the land mass at that time was thought to be only a few hundred miles, thus making Cortereall's geography somewhat askew. There was a passage across it, he said, and he called it the Straits of Anian.

It wasn't, necessarily, an out and out conspiracy, but others soon joined the search, probably more out of hope than any attempt to defraud or to distort history. An Italian geographer named Gestaldo seized on Cortereall's claim and said the straits were what separated North America from Asia. (Vitus Bering discovered such a strait many years later but it was not what either Cortereall or Gestaldo had envisioned.) So Cortereall's words, plus a little help from the hopeful, started the search for the Northwest Passage.

Near the end of that century, in 1592, one Apostolos Valerianos, a Greek in the employ of Spain who took the name Juan de Fuca, claimed he had discovered what we know today as the Strait of Juan de Fuca. Valerianos was convinced he had found the Northwest Passage and so reported it.

By the year 1596 cartographers began listing Juan de Fuca's strait on their charts, although no one else was able to locate it and historians couldn't truly honor his claim until an Englishman, Captain Charles William Barclay, verified it almost 200 years later.

The Great River of the West theory apparently first flowered in 1603 when another Spaniard, d'Aguilar, reported it as a possibility after an admiral with a real sense of imagination, Pedro Bartolemo de Ponte, claimed he sailed upriver from the Pacific into a lake and then via a series of rivers and lakes, emerged eventually into the Atlantic. This report was embellished with descriptions of adventures he had had with friendly natives in great cities along the way.

Another bit of wishful thinking, under the guise of reporting, came from a friar by the name of Urdaneta who also declared he had passed successfully by water from ocean to ocean.

The Spaniards were predominant along the West Coast of America at this time. Balboa had discovered the Isthmus of Panama in 1513 and the Spaniards soon began bulding ships there to explore north along the California coast.

The English began to compete with them and the Spaniards were tormented by an English pirate, Sir Francis Drake, who wreaked havoc on them in his ship the Golden Hind. Drake sailed boldly into the harbors, looted the Spanish ships, destroyed the masts on them and, when the Golden Hind was loaded down with silver and gold he ordered all the lighter, bulkier cargo tossed over the side to make way for more pirated loot.

The Spaniards he victimized fumed and, desperate for explanations that might save their own hides back home, came up with the idea that Drake had discovered the mysterious Northwest Passage and fled into it after his raids. It was easier to explain that way than to reveal their own ineptitude.

By the beginning of the Eighteenth Century most of the tales about the Straits of Anian were being changed over to stories about the Great River of the West. The Ourigan, some called it. The English didn't bother much about the name but they did offer 20,000 pounds sterling to any sea captain who found an inland passage to Hudsons Bay from the Pacific.

By then the Spanish explorations had extended as far north as Nootka, on Vancouver Island, while the Russians had settled in Alaska and were thinking of leapfrogging down to establish a colony in California—which they did later at Fort Ross, north of Bodega Bay.

Captain James Cook, the Britisher who was to come to his untimely end in Hawaii, sailed along the Oregon and Washington coast in March, 1778, named Cape Foulweather, but wrote in his log that no river existed. French explorers also made journeys in the same area in 1786 and 1791. In 1775 the Spaniard, Bruno Heceta, spotted the water of the Columbia raging at the bar, noted the river extending back an estimated 30 miles from it, named it San Roque but, somewhat inexplicably, retreated from it without any serious attempt at entry.

Thirteen years later John Meares, an English sea captain, also encountered the bar but like the Spaniard before him failed to navigate across it, recording "we can now with safety assert that there is no such river as the St. Roc (of the Spaniard, Heceta) exists as laid down on the Spanish charts." He then named the bay in that vicinity Deception Bay and the promontory to the north Cape Disappointment.

And on April 27, 1792, a rather arrogant British captain by the name of George Vancouver noticed signs of a major river yet scoffed at reports of a mighty stream and declared "no Northwest Passage exists."

If all of this seems inconsistent it is perhaps proof that the search for the fabled Straits of Anian or for the river some knew as Oregon was not as fervent as we have been led to believe. Politics was certainly involved and the English and the Spaniards were usually at cross purposes in their western explorations.

However, even as the sea search went on along the coast, things were happening inland. In 1766-67 Johnathan Carver, on a journey to Minnesota, began to speak of a great river which he had been told rose in the western mountains and emptied into the Pacific. Only a year earlier Robert Rogers, of Rogers Rangers fame, had petitioned King George III of England to be allowed to lead an overland expedition to locate "the Oregon River."

So the myths of the Straits of Anian and the Northwest Passage ended when the Yankee, Gray, who had earlier captained the first American vessel to circumnavigate the globe and was now engaged in a trading expedition, crossed the bar at the Columbia's mouth, proved the legends false but knit the truth of the Great River of the West into the fineweave of history.

Captain Vancouver, apprised of Gray's discovery, returned to the Columbia's mouth that fall and on October 20, 1792, anchored his flagship *Discovery* offshore and sent Lieutenant William R. Broughton in *H. M. S. Chatham* into the river and almost 100 miles upstream. It is said that Broughton desisted from journeying farther only because the Indians warned him of the rapids he would soon encounter and after that warning he retreated downstream.

There Lieutenant Broughton made another interesting discovery: a fur trading vessel named the *Jenny* which had been in the river for some time.

As in so many other events of that era mystery surrounds the 78-ton schooner which was under the command of James Baker. It supposedly had a sister ship, the *Ruby*, and the two had been trading up and down the coast under strict orders from their owner, an eccentric Englishman with the delightful name of Sidenham Teast, "to keep your routes and your instructions a profound secret and to have no intercourse with any ships, especially when you are making trade."

In view of these and other stories the legend of Konapee seems to have some credence. There are many tales of shipwrecks along the Northwest coast and certainly the later misadventures of vessels in these waters bear them out. The Spanish galleons were no less vulnerable to the treacherous currents and tides than their counterparts from other countries.

It is said that Konapee was one of four sailors who survived a wreck on Clatsop Beach. All were captured by the Indians but Konapee won favor with his captors because he was a skilled blacksmith who made weapons and ornaments for them from iron and copper salvaged from the wrecked vessel. After ingratiating himself in this manner he escaped in a canoe which he paddled upriver to Celilo where he met and married the daughter of an Indian chief. Their union produced a son, Soto, and Konapee himself became a chief among the Indians, as did his son in later years.

The sailors lot in those days was not an entirely happy one. Disease was common and there are stories of "cures" involving men being buried up to the neck in dirt to rid them of some of the maladies contracted while they were at sea. After months and years away from home, it seems possible some of them might have been willing to quit their wandering ways and settle for a home in the new land. Although the frequently wet and sometimes cold Columbia River Gorge suffers by comparison to the artists' conception of an earlier, Biblical Eden, it qualifies on counts of beauty and a bountiful food supply.

No records account for survivors of shipwrecks, those who made it

13

ashore, married into the tribes who captured them or which they joined. It appears they did produce some offspring and in that category there is Cullaby, said to be the son of an Indian, whom Lewis and Clark saw near the end of 1805 and who is mentioned in writing as a "well-known character on the Clatsop Plains," a man with a reddish beard deemed to be "certainly half white." There are a multitude of other tales, some of them as vague as whispers on the wind, but others appear to have substance.

Let us assume then, for the purpose of this narrative, that the legend of Konapee has some basis in fact and is not a fiction invented out of imagination, a tale to be told around campfires at night. Let us assume that the Spaniard was, indeed, hurled by Fate onto the North American shore near the mouth of the Columbia and lived many years in the Columbia Gorge.

He may, or may not, have been the first white man on the river and the first white man at Celilo. In legends "firsts" are second to the romantic quality involved and all the elements of romance—shipwreck, capture, escape, love, marriage, family and rise to power—are present in Konapee's story.

But, as in an earlier Eden, change was inevitable.

This book is an attempt to relate those changes, to recount the history of the physical alterations and to offer a guide to touring the still splendid scenery, including those things which exist from the past as well as those which are part of the still changing present. For all of these are what shaped the Gorge of the Columbia from those long ago days when it was the object of search and discovery by many nations—from the time before Konapee entered his Eden to the present. And these events, be they fact, fantasy or fable, are part of the mystique of the Columbia River Gorge.

The great migration . . .

The earliest explorations along the Northwest coast may have been in search of the Straits of Anian, or for gold, but reality had replaced these dreams and soon it was recognized that the "gold" in the area consisted of beaver fur—and title to the land itself.

The fur trappers of John Jacob Astor's Pacific Fur Company and others took care of the former, but the struggle for the land soon became a British-American problem. The empire builders always had the land in mind.

Although the Yankee ship captain, Gray, had discovered and named the Columbia, only five months later Lieutenant Broughton was laying claim to all the land in the vicinity and placing the names of Britons upon it—i.e., Mount Hood—while Captain Vancouver ignored Gray's prior presence and grandly took formal possession of the river and the land adjacent to it, "having every reason to believe, that the subjects of no other civilized nation or state had ever entered the river before."

Then Thomas Jefferson was elected president of the still young republic of the United State and in 1803 arranged to acquire from France the 805,000 square miles known as The Louisiana Purchase. Even after interest payments the original price of 60 million francs ($15,000,000) was about 4 cents per acre, but some feared the U.S. would never be able to lay legal claim to this vast region.

Jefferson organized the Lewis and Clark expedition to explore the territory, including the upper reaches of the Missouri River and thence beyond it to the coast, the latter goal being accomplished when the explorers reached the Pacific Ocean at the mouth of the Columbia on November 15, 1805. It was a journey replete with hardships but definitely in the grand American tradition.

Traveling through the Columbia Gorge, Lewis and Clark noted landmarks that still exist, although some names were changed by later settlers. Thus, what they knew as Castle Rock became Beacon Rock, what they called the Cataract River is now the Klickitat, Labieche's River became first the Dog River and is now the Hood River, Canoe Creek is known today as the White Salmon River and after spotting many seals at the mouth of another stream they named Seal River what is now known as the Washougal.

15

Lewis and Clark experienced difficulties in navigating through the Gorge, as did later explorers. One of the more interesting descriptions of a portion of their journey is contained in a book published in 1904 by Interstate Publishing Company, titled "An Illustrated History of Klickitat, Yakima and Kittitas Counties." Here is that account of Lewis and Clark's trip past the rapids and falls at Celilo: "After making several portages they reached that extraordinary place (now called The Dalles) where all the waters gathered from half a million square miles of earth are squeezed into a crack forty-five yards wide. The desolation on either side of this frightful chasm is a fitting margin. As one crawls to the edge and peeps over he sees the waters to be of inky blackness. Streaks of foam gridiron the blackness. There is little noise compared with that made by the shallow rapids above but rather a dismal sough, as though the rocks were rubbing their black sides together in a vain effort to close the escaping river. The river here is 'turned on edge.'"

However, according to this report, and to the amazement of the watching Indians, "Lewis and Clark, finding the roughness of the shore made it almost impossible to carry their boats over, and seeing no evidence of rocks in the channel, boldly steered through this 'witches cauldron.'"

(Nor was this to be their last bout with river rapids. Continuing on downstream they got past the Cascades "after two difficult portages" and are believed to have camped that night, November 9, 1805, near the base of what is now known as Rooster Rock.)

Lewis and Clark headed what was surely the most famous of all western American expeditions and were the forerunners of settlement and development of the Northwest territory. This exploration led to the coining of the slogan "Fifty-four forty or fight," and ultimately to the Americanization of the entire area of Oregon and Washington.

In 1810, John Jacob Astor, a German born immigrant who had already made a fortune by trading furs with the Indians in the eastern United States and Canada, formed the Pacific Fur Company, intending to compete with the British-Canadian companies in the Northwest. Thus the town named Astoria at the Columbia's mouth which was, for a short time, Astor's western headquarters.

Astor's foray into the new land, however, experienced a series of disasters and these, plus the War of 1812, caused him to sell his western holdings to The NorthWest Company which, in turn, was later taken over by the Hudsons Bay Company. Also, while the British occupied it, the town of Astoria was known as Fort George.

Even after the War of 1812 ended the Northwest country was still claimed by three nations: the United States, England and Spain. The latter, realizing their tenuous position, renounced claims to it in 1819, preferring to consolidate their hold on California.

For a time the British and Americans had an agreement for joint oc-

16

cupancy. But the Lewis and Clark expeditioin had fired the American imagination. The agreement soon began to founder when the great western migration of Americans began in 1840 and in 1846 the Oregon Treaty gave the United States title to the land presently within its boundaries. In 1848 the U.S. government established the Oregon Territory (although it took five months for word of it to reach the Northwest). This territory included all of Oregon and Washington as well as parts of Idaho, Montana and Wyoming.

To get some idea of the growth, the population of the Oregon Territory at the end of 1841 was put at 253, of whom only 35 were regarded as settlers. Another 111 persons arrived in 1842 and in 1843 Marcus Whitman brought 875 with him. Another 800 came west in 1844 and this number was swelled by an additional 3,000 in 1845.

Getting to the territory was a lengthy, arduous journey, and not all of those who made it could be classed as pioneers of the heroic mold in which we tend to cast them. Judge Bennett, in his book "Recollections of Old Pioneers," remarked: "Among the men who came to Oregon the year I did, some were idle, worthless young men, too lazy to work at home and too gentle to steal, while some were gamblers, and others reported thieves. But when we arrived in Oregon they were compelled to work. It was a bare necessity."

Thus the pioneer work ethic was established at the end, if not the beginning, of the long trek.

Many of these early arrivals, being opportunists, headed for California in 1849 when word got out that gold had been discovered there. But that outward migration was soon offset by another wave of land hungry settlers when Congress passed the Donation Land Act of 1850, giving large tracts of free land to those who settled in Oregon.

From the beginning a majority of those people came overland and thus most of them passed through the Columbia River Gorge, for it was the only water level passage through the Cascade Range. So the Gorge became the funnel through which they poured, just as did the "waters gathered from half a million square miles of earth."

Not many of these travelers were impressed with Konapee's Eden. They were nearing the end of a journey which may have covered 2,000 miles or more, over a period of many months, and any impediment to their passage was considered with displeasure.

By the early 1850s the deluge was overwhelming. In the fall of 1852 the commanding officer at Fort Dalles recorded: "1,500 wagons, or 6,000 souls have arrived at this point and about 600 more wagons are to follow."

These settlers, eager to reach the potential farmlands beyond the Gorge, had little use for Indians and no thought was given to native rights as first claimants to the territory. The new immigrants brought with them

17

not only guns, livestock and tools with which to tame the land but their own particular heritage, including the white man's diseases to which the Indians were extremely vulnerable. In the year 1853 a smallpox epidemic killed 150 Indians at Wishram and the western "trading mart" was closed as other Indians feared to come to it.

So a civilization which had nurtured the Indians for more than 10,000 years was coming to an end as the oldest settlement on the North American continent was downgraded to the point where the site was regarded mostly as an inconvenience barring the way to the white settlers goal.

The Indians, outnumbered by the new arrivals, wracked by their diseases, scorned and pushed aside as indigent thieves or "hostiles", could only watch this invasion with dismay.

Konapee's Eden had undergone the greatest change since it had been created in the years following the the Ice Age.

Artist Jimmie James, 77, used charcoals from old Indian fires for this sketch of the legendary Bridge of the Gods. *Photo courtesy Oregon Historical Society.*

Eliminating impediments
on the broad highway . . .

Interstate-84, part of the national network of 4-lane highways, parallels the Columbia River along the south shore of the Gorge while the 2-lane Washington State Highway 14 does the same on the north shore. In addition to these means of passage the Burlington Northern Railroad sends trains along its tracks on the north shore while the Union Pacific route runs along the south shore. In the river itself barges shepherd cargo upstream, through the locks at Bonneville Dam, beneath the modern day Bridge of the Gods and through locks at succeeding dams all the way to Lewiston, Idaho.

A traveler, whizzing down either of the 2 highways, is confronted constantly by a multitude of vistas, both of the river and the great, brooding cliffs or the mountains rising toward the sky. Today's traveler may not realize that in the early years the river itself was the broad highway through the Gorge, the chief passageway for explorers and settlers intent on reaching their goal. These trailblazers saw the picturesque rapids and falls in the Columbia as impediments that must somehow be overcome.

The horseshoe-shaped falls at Celilo and the community of The Dalles that grew up nearby were to mark the end of the overland route via the Oregon Trail. Getting past the long stretch of rapids and falls required extra effort, but beyond the Long Narrows and Big Eddy the hills and cliffs crowded ever closer to the waters edge and the trees grew thick and tall. The last barrier in the river between the travelers and their destinations was the Cascades, a two and one-half mile stretch of rapids created, according to legend, when the rock arch that had once spanned the river— the original Bridge of the Gods—collapsed.

It was these rapids the Indians had warned Lieutenant Broughton about and, heeding their words, he had turned back. Later explorers pushed relentlessly upstream from the river's mouth to be met at the Cascades by the fractious natives who lived there.

Among these exlporers was Alexander Ross, who in July, 1811, reached the Cascades as he headed eastward and remarked: "From this point we examined the road over which we had to transport goods and found it to be 1,450 yards long, with a steep descent near the Indian villages, at the end, with up and down hills, gullies, and thick woods from one end to end. To say there is not a worse path under the sun would be going a step

19

too far, but to say that for difficulty and danger few could equal it, would be saying but the truth. Certainly nothing could be more discouraging than our present situation: obstacles on every side, by land, by water, and from the Indians, all hostile alike."

The natives at the Cascades numbered between 250 and 300 and were, in Ross's words, "lazy rascals, who attempted to annoy us in every kind of way—break our canoes, pilfer our property and even threaten ourselves by throwing stones and pointing arrows at us."

Early travelers dreaded these Indians more than any other along the river and many harrowing tales are told of journeys both upstream and down past this major obstacle.

As the flood tide of settlers increased it became apparent a better method must be found to get past the rapids. In 1851 Frances H. Chenowith, an attorney from Wisconsin who had come west in 1849 to claim land on the north shore of the river, started a store at the Lower Cascades. After eyeing the narrow, muddy, slippery two-mile long trail he decided to build, with J. A. Bush, a wooden tramway.

A mule, walking a plank between the wooden rails, drew a small flat car along this route and the charge was 75 cents per 100 pounds of cargo. Most passengers preferred to walk, with only their belongings loaded on the tram.

Two years later Chenowith sold out to the Bradford Brothers (Bush retained his interest) and the tramway was extended to a total length of 6 miles.

In 1850 the population of the territory was put at 13,294, of which 1,049 lived north of the river. Shortly thereafter the area at the Cascades became a shipbuilding center, although it was said there were only 4 white adults and 2 small boys living at the side of Cascade Locks while 2 white adults and 2 children lived across the river at Stevenson.

Still, in the mid-1850s, men working with hand tools built the steamboats *Mary* and *Wasco* and by 1857 the sternwheeler *Hassalo*. Lumber was obtained from a sawmill powered by an overshot waterwheel, with logs brought to it by six or twelve yoke ox teams.

The Indians remained unfriendly, however, and in time their dissatisfaction with the white intruders spread over a greater area. A major uprising, in 1856, was centered primarily on the north shore near the Cascades.

One family caught up in the Indian war was that of Erastus Joslyn. Joslyn, born in Massachusetts, had married Mary Warner in 1848 and arrived in Oregon in 1852 after a trip across the Isthmus of Panama. He settled in what is now Bingen and was for a time the only white settler east of the Cascades on the north side of the Columbia.

Joslyn and his family escaped personal injury only because a friendly native by the name of Sapitowell disclosed to them the Indian plot to

Running the Cascades became a spectator sport, as crowds lined the shore to watch the steamship Hassalo go through the rapids on May 26, 1888, with Captain Jas. Troup at the wheel. *Hofsteater Photo courtesy Oregon Historical Society.*

murder the family and destroy their home. Joslyn took his wife to the Cascades where she remained with Mrs. Attwell, whose home was on the south shore, while Joslyn went to conduct business in The Dalles.

Later, when the Indians attacked the Attwell home, Mrs. Joslyn escaped with the Attwell family aboard the steamboat *Mary*, which appropriated the Attwell's cedar rail fence for fuel to aid in the upriver flight.

As a result of his actions in warning the Joslyns Sapitowell was regarded as a traitor by the other Indians, who vowed to kill him. So he remained with the whites he had befriended and eventually changed his name to Charles Johnson.

Joslyn returned to the north shore when the war ended and although General Wool had decreed no whites were to live east of the Cascades north of the river he exempted the Joslyn family from that order because they had settled their Bingen claim prior to the uprising. In 1858 General Clark rescinded Wool's order and the eastward movement along the north shore began.

Joslyn later represented Skamania County in the Washington Territorial Legislature, but moved from the Northwest to Colorado in 1875 and then to Santa Barbara some years later. He died in the latter city in 1904.

Still, even after the Indian war the Cascades remained a barrier to river traffic, the importance of which loomed larger daily. Although the federal government decided, in 1875, to adopt a plan for permanent improvement they moved towards fulfillment of that promise with typical bureaucratic footdragging.

The steamboats were out on the river in force now, hauling cargo and people both up and down stream, and the north shore portage at the Cascades became so expensive that it was known for a time as "Racket Road."

In 1881 the State of Oregon built a portage road around the rapids on the south bank, to control prices, and the first year in operation this road handled ten thousand tons of freight and eight thousand passengers.

The federal government's plan to create locks was finally completed in 1896 and they bypassed the rapids entirely. At that time the navigation tracks on the south portage were taken up and the locomotive and cars were sold. The community around the completed project was, and is, known as Cascade Locks.

With the completion of these locks there began a campaign upriver at The Dalles to get some water bypass for Celilo Falls. Riverboat operators complained that the railroads, now completed, were monopolizing shipping and soon, in 1903, Celilo Locks and canal were authorized and completed in 1915 at a cost of 4.5 million dollars. It was eight and a half miles long, sixty-five feet wide, with turnouts to enable boats to pass each other.

Of this project writer Steward Holbook said: "It was the ultimate fantasy of Federal spending at its worst." By 1920 the canal and locks were virtually idle, for the railroads still hauled the freight and the Scenic Highway, completed while the canal was under construction, was furnishing an available ground route for people who owned automobiles. Holbrook remarked that when he viewed the canal in 1923 he was told by a friend at The Dalles that no craft had passed through the locks in the last 3 months.

However, the canal was used later as steel barges drawn by propeller-driven tugboats began to haul wheat downriver and oil and gasoline started to move upstream in special barges.

The great depression of the 1930s created an interest by the Federal government to start construction projects in the Northwest. One was Bonneville Dam, which was authorized by President Roosevelt in 1933 and completed in 1939.

Prior to the time the dam was built the railroad maintained a popular eating house at the eventual dam site and for many years this area was one of the favorite picnic grounds for residents along the Columbia River between The Dalles and Portland.

The community had been named for Captain Benjamin L. E. Bonneville, made famous by Washington Irving's *The Adventures of Captain Bonneville*. The Captain (later General) was born in France in 1795, came to the United States, graduated from West Point and fought in the Mexican War. He explored much of the western United States in the period 1832-35, visiting many parts of Oregon. It is believed he may have been the first white man to enter the Wallowa Mountain country in eastern Oregon.

Thus the Cascades were subdued, first by wooden tramway along the shore, then by locks and finally by innundation. When The Dalles Dam was completed in the 1950s Celilo Falls also disappeared and when the gates to the John Day Dam were closed in 1968 and water began to be impounded behind them the full utilization of the Columbia River for navigation far into the western interior was realized. Only one short stretch of it between the Canadian border and Bonneville remains unfettered.

In less than 300 years Konapee's Eden had been transformed into its present day version. In the process of transition many scenic views were obliterated and the historic value of artifacts buried beneath the water is incalculable. And while many go hungry in the world each night the great salmon runs have been decimated to the point where the fish in now a luxury item in restaurants and grocery stores.

The price of eliminating the difficulties of river transport and creating megawatts of power to light the Northwest cities has been paid as the once vibrant river was turned into a lake to fit the needs of modern civilization.

Still, along the banks of the river in the Columbia Gorge the tower-

This 1899 picture shows salmon jumping rapids above The Dalles. *Photo courtesy Oregon Historical Society.*

ing basaltic cliffs and the mountains beyond them watch over it, waiting for more changes yet to come. The nature of these changes, and their effect on the Gorge, is yet to be determined.

Sam Hill (right) shown here with C. C. Colt and Henry S. Groves, in 1915, played a prominent role in the creation of the Scenic Highway. *Photo courtesy Oregon Historical Society.*

Roadside & Other Attractions I

The Scenic Highway *(Western section)*

Interstate 84 remains as the quickest way to travel the length of the Columbia River Gorge, but for those interested in scenic values a 22-mile journey along the western section of the historic Columbia River Scenic Highway offers rewards not obtained by racing along the freeway.

For the eastbound the Scenic Highway tour begins at Lewis and Clark State Park, just after crossing the Sandy River, or at the 2 exits immediately prior to it. Westbound travelers will find Scenic Highway exit signs west of Bonneville and before Multnomah Falls. The tour as described here is conducted west to east.

But first, a bit of history.

By the dawn of the Twentieth Century advances in technology demanded a means of land transport through the Gorge. The automobile had arrived and there was frustration at not being able to drive from Portland to The Dalles.

Road building attempts had begun as early as 1856 when a short wagon road around the Cascades had been completed. In 1862 Brigadier General Rufus Ingalls stressed the need for "having a good wagon road from Vancouver to The Dalles, probably passing the Cascade Mountains on the Oregon side of the Columbia."

However, despite continuing efforts, one using convict labor, it was 1915 before success at a through route was attained. The creation of the Columbia River Scenic Highway ranks as one of the major engineering achievements in the world at that time.

The highway came into being because of the combined efforts of many men. Chief among them were wealthy entrepreneur Samuel Hill, an ardent advocate of good roads; Samuel Lancaster, Hill's protegee, who served as Consulting Engineer; Simon Benson, Portland lumberman and lover of the Gorge and John B. Yeon, another Portlander who donated more than 2 years of his time to serve as roadmaster for the project.

Hill was the driving force. A Seattleite who owned a large tract of land on the north shore of the Columbia, east of Wishram, he had become acquainted with Lancaster and was impressed with his abilities. In 1908 he invited the engineer to accompany him to Europe to study some of the highways on the continent. A brief 5 years later work was begun on the Scenic Highway.

27

It was a task which seemed foredoomed to failure, despite the coterie of brilliant and dedicated engineers who joined in the effort. The specifications for the road were for a minimum width of 24 feet, with extra width on all curves, no turn radius less than 100 feet and a maximum grade of 5 percent.

Just how difficult these specifications were to meet can be understood only by knowing that along some sections of the proposed route previous tries at road building had resulted in grades up to a maximum of 20 percent. Lancaster and his engineers were sorely tried to meet the specifications.

But meet them they did, and along the way they created a marvelous series of view points, viaducts and tunnels, many of which, regrettably, were destroyed by later generations.

The effort inspired volunteer labor crews, in addition to the regular workers, and several public spirited citizens made land donations. The result of the latter was picnic areas and parks to add enjoyment to the trip.

Simon Benson purchased 300 acres of land, including Multnomah Falls and Wahkeena Falls, and donated them to the state, while George Shepperd gave 11 acres at Shepherd's Dell, in memory of his wife. Several other donations were made in later years.

The Scenic Highway tour begins, as stated, at the Sandy River, and the road parallels the east bank of it for a short distance.

The Sandy is a popular summer swimming spot and in the spring is subject to one of the better smelt runs in the Northwest, where dip netters turn out in force to harvest this silvery little fish.

The Sandy was named the Quicksand River by Lewis and Clark and, prior to that, the Barings River by Lieutenant Broughton. (Lewis and Clark camped on a prairie opposite the Sandy on their homeward bound trip in 1806 and an historical marker at Lewis and Clark State Park summarizes their interesting experiences here).

It is just under 2.5 miles from the freeway exit to Dabney State Park, which is available for both picnics and over-night camping. Boat ramps to the Sandy are also in the park.

From this point eastward the Scenic Highway becomes, at times, a journey through a modern Eden which still holds a certain primeval charm and offers innumerable remarkable vistas and experiences. It climbs steadily, passing through the hamlet of Springdale and then the village of Corbett, which was named for Senator Henry Winslow Corbett, who owned a farm nearby.

Two miles past Corbett the road reaches Chanticleer Point, from which the first great upriver view is obtainable. Chanticleer Point was so named by Mr. and Mrs. A. H. Morgan when they built a resort on the

Columbia River Highway, 1915. *Photo courtesy Oregon Historical Society.*

site in 1912. This building was destroyed by fire in 1931. In 1956 the Portland Women's Forum purchased 3.7 acres and donated it to the State Park system. The park is a popular spot for photographers as the unique Vista House atop Crown Point is clearly visible about 1 mile to the east.

The Scenic Highway descends slightly en route to Crown Point and the stone walls along the highway begin to become evident. These walls were built by Italian laborers who used neither cement nor mortar, following the example of similar walls along some of the European roads, and they led one observer to dub the highway "a poem in stone".

Crown Point is the remains of a basalt flow some 25 million years ago. It is believed the flow completely filled the canyon at that time but all except this promontory was swept away in the great floods. Rooster Rock, alongside the freeway below, is a portion that broke off and slid down to the canyon floor in fairly recent times, geologically speaking. The large rock formation visible in the distance on the north shore is Beacon Rock.

Descending from Crown Point the highway loops gracefully down to near river level, passing in the process many of the major waterfalls in this part of the Gorge which are, sucessively, Latourell, Bridal Veil, Shepperd's Dell, Wahkeena, Multnomah and Horsetail. These spectacular falls spill over the top of the basalt flows which formed the great cliffs along the south shore and each of them, except Bridal Veil, has parking areas from which the falls may be viewed and photographed. A complex system of trails allows adventure for those who wish to explore away from the roadside.

(Those who decide to journey any substantial distance on foot should first acquire either a book detailing these trails or U.S.G.S. maps. Many of the trails interlock and it is possible to wander far away if the wrong turn is taken).

Guy W. Talbot State Park, a picnic area, is across the highway from Latourell Falls, which is 12 miles from the I-84 exit. An early railroad station here was named for a prominent settler and postmaster, Joseph Latourell. The falls are on property once owned by Talbot and for many years the vicinity was known as "Talbot's Place." In 1929 the Talbots gave 220 acres, including the falls, to the State of Oregon.

Latourell Falls can best be seen from a viewpoint on the south side of the highway just after crossing the bridge over the creek. A walk leads down to the base of the falls, then turns north and follows the creek under the highway to the picnic area.

The name for Bridal Veil Falls presumably comes from some romantic connation, but no view is offered here because the road passes directly over the top of them.

At Shepperd's Dell a lovely stone walkway leads down to the falls midpoint. Parking space is available at the east end of the bridge.

Wahkeena is said to be an Indian word meaning "most beautiful," and

Wahkeena Falls are unique in that they more closely resemble a true cascade, as the water tumbles down over steeply slanted rocks, rather than the sheer drop in the other Gorge falls.

The Mazamas, an Oregon outdoor hiking and mountain climbing group, gave the falls this name in 1915. Prior to that time it was known as Gordon Falls. A large picnic area adjoins the north side of the highway, opposite the falls.

The height of the 2 drops at Multnomah Falls totals 620 feet, although some of the very early estimates placed them, erroneously, as "near 1,000 feet." Curiously, none of the explorers along the Columbia appear to have applied any name to them although virtually all made mention of this largest fall in the Gorge. The name Multnomah Falls is believed to have originated in the 1860s with the idea of popularizing them as a point along the river during steamboat excursions, which were much in vogue at that time.

Multnomah Falls Lodge is an impressive and handsome structure built by the City of Portland in 1925 and donated to the Federal government in 1943. It is operated by permit issued by the Forest Service and offers snacks, meals and souvenirs as well as a spot from which to begin the walk part way or all the way to the top of Multnomah Falls.

East of Multnomah Falls the Scenic Highway is carried on a viaduct for a short distance before arriving at Oneonta Gorge, a narrow fissure in the rocks through which courses Oneonta Creek. It is believed the name comes from the New York State town of the same name.

Horsetail Falls, the last of the falls along this tour, is a descriptive term which has been in use since the early days. The falls are so close to the road that a fine mist sprays across it. For a somewhat unusual experience take the trail here for a short hike which enables you to walk *behind* upper Horsetail Falls as the trail leads along the base of a cliff over which these falls plunge.

East of Horsetail is the entrance to Ainsworth State Park, named for a pioneer Oregon citizen, Captain J.C. Ainsworth. The land for the park was donated by his heirs.

Great basaltic cliffs and formations tower over Ainsworth Park and overnight campers can sit around their campfires at the base of these giants which bear names like St. Peter's Dome and Rock of Ages.

St. Peter's Dome is a basalt monolith originally known as Cathedral Rock. It was challenged for many years by mountain climbers before the summit was reached in 1940 by a party of 6, including Joe Leuthold and Ida Darr.

About a mile past the park the Scenic Highway re-connects with Interstate-84.

Roadside & Other Attractions II

Interstate-84, Sandy River to Panorama Point

This tour description is designed to point out those things which can be seen through the automobile window as you drive past them as well as suggestions for point of interest stops and some history for background. The tour begins as I-84 crosses the Sandy River, headed east.

As mentioned earlier, Lewis and Clark are believed to have spent a night at the base of Rooster Rock. The landmark is now the site of Rooster Rock State Park and in the summer, if the Columbia's flow is low enough, it is probably *the* most popular bathing beach along the river and certainly in the Gorge.

Rooster Rock has undergone a series of names changes. The term The Obelisk never found popular favor. Cock Rock was an obvious reference to the phallic significance — too obvious for some sensibilities — and so the substitute name Rooster Rock came into popular usage.

For a car window view of the Vista House at Crown Point glance up to the south as you pass Rooster Rock. Farther on, approaching Multnomah Falls, a look high up along the cliff above Benson State Park will reveal Mist Falls, a very minor stream which has a sheer drop of some distance and the Gorge winds sometimes blow with such velocity that the waterfall literally disappears in mid-drop.

Multnomah Falls can also be reached from I-84. A large parking lot is available. Some of the other waterfalls can be glimpsed from the freeway, but the trees are growing up to the extent that visibility is being constantly decreased. Fortunately St. Peter's Dome, Rock of Ages and others in that group towering over Ainsworth State Park rise to such heights that they can be seen clearly.

Just after the point where the Scenic Highway rejoins I-84, the names Dodson and Warrendale appear on road signs, and both indicate settlements now virtually extinct. The Dodson station was named for Ira Dodson, an early settler. Warrendale was once a post office serving the territory west of Bonneville. The name is for Frank M. Warren, Sr., a pioneer citizen of Portland who was drowned in the wreck of the *Titanic* in April, 1912.

The next exit east is to Bonneville Dam, which the U.S. Army Corps

Lower Eagle Creek Trail. This entire trail, built about 1915, is still used extensively. *Photo courtesy Oregon Historical Society.*

of Engineers has turned into a showplace. There are extensive lawns and a large visitors center. A trip downstairs in the latter offers an excellent underwater view of the salmon and other fish migrating upstream via the fish ladders. Outside viewing of these ladders is available, too.

On the return trip to the freeway a worthwhile stop is at the Oregon State Fish Hatchery, where thousands of fingerling salmon darken the waters of the holding tanks prior to their release into the river. A trout pond and sturgeon pond give excellent views of fine specimens of each of these fish and there are a number of displays in buildings which give a detailed history of Oregon fish.

One mile east of the Bonneville Dam exit, and immediately after the freeway passes through a short tunnel, the Eagle Creek Exit at Milepost 41 leads to one of the unique areas in the Gorge and its most famous hiking trail.

The bridge over Eagle Creek was one of the most beautiful along the Scenic Highway, a full-centered arch of re-inforced concrete faced with native stone. A turn to the left after crossing this bridge leads under the freeway to a parking lot at the foot of a small hill, atop which sits Overlook Park, a picnic area containing a shelter house which was supposedly built to house some of the flora species found in the Eagle Creek area.

At the time the Scenic Highway was constructed around 1915 the Eagle Creek Trail was also being built. At that time the Forest Service opened up a fossil bed which attracted national attention, for it contained many genera and species now extinct.

The drive to the Eagle Creek trailhead is less than a mile — right turn after crossing the Eagle Creek Bridge — along a road paralleling the creek. The trail leads eventually to Wahtum Lake, 13 miles up in the mountains, but it is only a 1.5 mile hike to Metlako Falls or 2 miles to The Punchbowl, the latter a photographers delight. (Handholding of small children along portions of this trail is advised.)

There is also a fish hatchery and a Forest Service campground at Eagle Creek. From the latter a walk of less than a mile along the Ruckel Creek Trail leads to a stone bridge over Ruckel Creek and a chance to wander along a short stretch of the Scenic Highway, now abandoned and covered with moss, with the trees arching their branches overhead.

Ruckel Creek presumably was named for Joseph Ruckel, who left New York in 1845 and spent some time in San Francisco before moving to Oregon in 1855. There he took a homestead upriver from Eagle Creek and later joined with his neighbor, Harrison Olmstead, to engage in river steamboat traffic.

Exit 44 is to the community of Cascade Locks where the locks are now designated as a National Historic Site. The Port of Cascade Locks has developed a park and a marina, and a museum contained in an old house exhibits local history. Here also is the Oregon Pony, the first steam engine used in the Northwest.

Tourists can watch as fishermen back their campers up to the old locks and set out their lines; can drive across the north shore via the modern day Bridge of the Gods, a steel span crossing the Columbia, or take a river cruise.

The latter is made possible by the Port's 300-ton *Columbia Gorge Sternwheeler*. The boat, built to revive memories of days of yore, offers excursions 7 days a week, with additional boardings at Bonneville Dam and Stevenson, Washington, from Memorial Day through September.

East of Cascade Locks, between Mileposts 48 and 49, is an overhead sign advising Slide Area and the possibility of slides continues through Milepost 52 near Shellrock Mountain. This is one of the few places on the south shore where the exposed rock is not basalt but diorite, a coarse grained rock densely speckled with white crystals of plagioclase feldspar. Big piles of this shattered rock crowd down to the highway and a look up the side of the mountain reveals a small portion of what appears at first to be a rock wall but which is, in fact, the remains of one of the earliest road building attempts in the area.

The bedrock here consists of an ancient basalt flow, topped by tropical soils which were, in turn, covered by a later basalt flow. The soils which form the middle layer tend to push up through this later flow, causing the top layer to slide and the result is an almost perpetual repair job on the highway.

Exit 51 denotes Wyeth, a former railroad station which was for a number of years the site of a railroad tie creosoting plant. Nathaniel Wyeth, one of the Oregon Territory's outstanding patriots and traders, crossed overland to the Willamette Valley in 1832, the first American to make that journey since the Astor Expedition's Wilson Price Hunt party. Wyeth established Fort William, a trading post, on Sauvies Island, and was a friend of J.K. Townsend and Thomas Nuttall, who were pioneer Oregon scientists.

Three miles east of the Wyeth exit, at Milepost 54, a look out the window to the right reveals a glimpse of 2 waterfalls. The first of these is a high, delicate ribbon cascade which was recently named Lancaster Falls, after the consulting engineer for the Scenic Highway.

The second is an oddity, a waterfall gushing out the middle of a cliff. Known technically as Warren Creek Falls it has earned the popular sobriquet "Hole-In-The-Wall-Falls." A diversion tunnel through the cliff was built to alleviate a rock hazard that was created periodically when the waters of Warren Creek became impounded at the top of the cliff by an accumulation of loose rock during low water periods. When the rains came the water would exert enough force to flush these rocks out and across the highway below.

35

Starvation Creek Park (Milepost 55) is a complete misnomer, an exercise in exaggeration, for no one is known to have starved here. The name is the result of an incident in December, 1884, a year after the railroad was completed. That month 2 trains were snowbound and it is said that men on skis packed food in from Hood River to feed the passengers, and that the railroad offered the passengers 3 dollars per day to shovel snow. The name Starveout was originally applied to the area.

Starvation Creek is the last of the major Gorge waterfalls. It is a picnic and rest area and a wooden bridge across the creek leads to the base of the falls. Another short section of the Scenic Highway can also be seen east of the rest rooms.

A walk back along the fence beside the exit road (available for eastbound travelers only) will pass Cabin Creek Falls, a roaring springtime torrent that dwindles to a wispy whisper in the dry days of summer. A portion of the Scenic Highway roadbed soon turns into a path through the woods which then emerges into an open area from which can be viewed both Lancaster and Hole-In-The-Wall-Falls.

For those who wish to experience camping in the Gorge overnight, Exit 56 is to Viento State Park, a modern facility. The name Viento is believed to come from the first two letters of three railroad men — Villard, Endicott and Tolman. It is perhaps coincidental that viento is also a Spanish word meaning wind, which is a constant factor in this section of the Gorge.

Just after Viento Park, at Milepost 58, is an exit to Lausman Park. This remains undeveloped, but it does offer an excellent across-the-Columbia view of the famous Broughton Flume.

Exit 64 is to Highway 35 along the east edge of the city of Hood River. Turn right after exiting and follow the signs to Panorama Point from which the mountains and the Hood River Valley can be seen from a small pinnacle. Particularly in the spring, when the orchards are in bloom, is this stop a *must*, but it is well worth a visit any time of the year.

William Broughton, Lieutenant in Captain Vancouver's fleet, first sighted this "distant high snowy mountain" on October 29, 1792, and named it for Lord Samuel Hood, member of the British Board of Admiralty. *This R. I. Gifford photo courtesy Oregon Historical Society.*

Hood River

When Lord Samuel Hood, a member of the British Board of admiralty, signed the original instructions for Captain George Vancouver's voyage to America's Northwest Coast he unknowingly won for himself a measure of fame beyond that which he earned as a member of the Royal Navy, in which he served with distinction for more than half a century, beginning in 1741.

For when, on October 29, 1792, Lieutenant Broughton sighted "a very distant high snowy mountain....rising beautifully conspicuous in the midst of an extensive tract of low, or moderately elevated land....." and then repeated this sighting the following day he, in Captain Vancouver's words, "honored it with Lord Hood's name."

Unlike so many of the place names which were changed at least once by succeeding explorers or settlers, the original appellation for the mountain has remained, thus perpetuating Lord Hood's name in the new republic which had but recently won its independence from England.

The early travelers were not as impressed with mountains as we are today. Back then they were used as landmarks instead of recreation areas. Only one major challenge has been issued to the name Mount Hood, that from Hall J. Kelley who, in 1834, led a campaign to call the Cascade Range the Presidents Range, with each peak named after the last name of a former U.S. President.

As time passed the name of the mountain begat other names. Thus Hood River, which in reality is 2 rivers, the East Fork and the West Fork, before they merge just south of Hood River, the second largest city in the Columbia River Gorge and the largest city in Hood River, the county.

(The river survived 2 name changes. Lewis and Clark called it Labiche — some spelled it Labeasche — and for a short time it was known as Dog River, because some starving travelers ate dog meat in the vicinity in early pioneer times).

Perhaps it is the common name, applied to a number of different places, which makes this area unique. Or perhaps it is because it is also a dividing line between east and west in the Columbia River Gorge, as the narrow canyon containing the mighty river opens up for the first time since the Sandy River. Climatically there is also a considerable difference as the rain west of this point makes the forest and undergrowth more dense and lush and the drier air to the east creates a more sparse and sometimes barren atmosphere.

The Hood River Valley was not a trouble spot in the early days, as was The Dalles and the Cascades, and so it escaped much of the notoriety of the Indian war and other diversions of that time. The early river travelers, having successfully passed The Dalles, were quite content to take advantage of the free flowing river for as long as possible before they arrived at the next barrier to downstream progress.

It is known that Lewis and Clark were in the valley for a little while, as were the fur trappers, but Nathaniel Coe is credited with being the first permanent white settler, filing a Land Donation Claim in 1854. And it was Coe who arranged for Hood River's rendevous with destiny by planting the first fruit tree.

Other settlers planted more fruit trees until, by 1890, the words "Hood River" and "apples" were synonymous in Oregon. The bitter cold winter of 1919 featured a freeze that spelled near disaster for the valley growers, however, and in an attempt to prevent a repetition of it they opted for variety, adding cherry and pear trees to the apples that remained in their orchards. Now, in the spring, the valley is a mass of pink and white blossoms while in the summer and fall the bounty is harvested. These fruits are shipped, fresh and canned, all over the world.

To add to the variety some are fermented into wine at the Mount Hood Winery, located 14 miles south of the city of Hood River on Woodworth Road, 1 mile west off Highway 35.

The winery, operated by Lester and Janis Martin, specializes in fruit and berry wines which they make semi-dry, as Martin avers that many fruit and berry wines are made sweet only to cover up the lack of quality in their creation. So he avoids sweetness in most of his vintages, excepting black cherry, which demands it.

The winery's tasting room opens onto a deck which overlooks the East Fork of the Hood River. Out front a rope dangles from a tall pole atop of which sits an old fashioned iron bell. The sign reads "Ring Bell for Service." Inside the tasting room are antiques and stained glass and an old but still operable Edison cylinder phonograph.

Lester Martin is a Wisconsin native and refugee from California who came to the valley to start his small but efficient winery. As with many on the Hood River scene he is an individualist.

The city of Hood River and the valley are alive with tales of earlier day characters, of wayward or lazy sons sent "out west" by irate parents with the message to "sink or swim" and the sons triumphing by amassing fortunes which sometimes equalled or surpassed that of their parents.

Nor are these stories confined to members of the male gender. Among the local legends is one regarding a lady of considerable means who escaped from an eastern city with her fortune intact after rousing her parents ire by marrying a family servant. On one of the mountains which form the bowl in which the Hood River Valley nestles she built a veritable castle and lived there with her husband for a number of years. According to legend, whenever she journeyed into the city — dressed in a green riding habit and driving a matched pair of white horses — she first locked her spouse in an upstairs bedroom!

But the charm of Hood River lies in more than the fruit in the valley or the characters who inhabit it. There is, for instance, the overwhelming presence of not one but two mountains. At the south end of the valley rises the north face of Lord Hood's peak, which has been called one of the the most beautiful mountains in the world, while 33 miles north of the Columbia the massive bulk of Mount Adams — sometimes referred to as "the forgotten giant" — appears from a distance to rise out of the river itself.

Once seen, these mighty mountains demand awareness, even when the clouds conceal them from view, for each stands well over 2 miles above sea level and they tower over the city and the valley like gigantic guardians.

In the legends of the Columbia River Indians, Mount Adams, Mount Hood and Mount St. Helens smoked continuously. The Indians called Adams and Hood brother mountains, naming them Pahto (or Paddo) and Wyeast, respectively, and according to this ancient scenario they both courted La-wa-la-clough (St. Helens), the fair damsel. When she expressed a preference for Adams, Hood flattened his northern brother's skull with a mighty blow, so that Adams never again dared to lift his head with pride.

The white man's history of Mount Adams is equally interesting. Captain Vancouver's party never advanced up the Columbia far enough to sight it and although Lewis and Clark spotted it in 1805 they made no attempt to name it as they confused it with St. Helens.

This confusion continued in later years when Hall J. Kelley's campaign to rename all the mountains in the Cascade Range was in full swing. Under Kelley's plan Hood's name was to be changed to Adams and St. Helen's to Washington.

Maps at that time were generally inadequate and one Thomas Farnham accidentally interchanged Kelley's names for Hood and St. Helens and then made a major error in latitude and placed the re-christened "Adams" about 40 miles east of St. Helens.

Stephen Harris writes in his book, FIRE AND ICE: "As Mountaineer Roy Smutek recently commented, 'In what has to be one of geography's greatest coincidences, there was a mountain there to accept the name.'"

So Kelley's scheme did not go entirely to waste, even if the only name that "took" was applied to a mountain whose existence he did not even

Picking the crop. *Photo courtesy Oregon Historical Society.*

suspect.

Although not included as one of the regular tours in this recital, there is a 23-mile scenic drive around the valley that is enjoyable, and particularly pleasing when the valley is in bloom or when the ripe fruit hangs heavy on the trees and roadside stands are set up to peddle it to passersby.

Start south from I-84 on Highway 35 and turn off it to go through the town of Odell.

This town was named for William Odell, who settled near here in 1881. His son, Milton Odell, was the first white child to be born in the valley and when the post office was established in 1910 it was called Newtown but changed to Odell the following year.

Take Highway 282 north from Odell to the intersection with 281, go south on the latter, along the West Fork of the Hood River to the town of Dee, which was established in 1906 and named for lumberman Thomas D. Dee.

Continue south to Parkdale, which town was established about 1910. The name seems to be self explanatory. The highway soon re-connects with 35 and the return north to I-84 is through the tiny community of Mount Hood where the Martin's winery is located.

Many, many side trips can be made from this little excursion and a passel of county parks and campgrounds are available for the enjoyment of anyone who has the time to spend in the valley.

Within this circle are many of the orchards as well as lumber mills, lumbering being also a major part of the economy. Beyond the circle and south of Parkdale the land becomes forested and rises toward Mount Hood as the air takes on a different quality, scented with pine and fir.

For persons so inclined another Hood River legend is worth checking out. In its own way the Columbia River Gorge Hotel is as much a part of the local lore as the wayward sons or the lady in the green riding habit.

It was the brainchild of Simon Benson, whose love for the Gorge has been chronicled earlier in this narrative. In 1921 he spent half a million dollars— a princely sum in those days — to build a tourist resort on a cliff above the river. It is located on Westcliff Drive, just north of the freeway.

The hotel was and is known for its extensive, park like grounds. The first manager of it was Henry Thiele, a name still famous in Portland restaurant circles, and early guests to the luxurious resort included social and political notables as well as film stars from the new but burgeoning movie industry in California.

The manicured grounds have been preserved, Wah-Gwin Falls still tumble over the boulders behind the hotel, each room is unique, the dinners sumptuous, the service superb, the farm breakfast staggering. A weekend stay stirs memories of halcyon days long gone, of graces forgotten, of gentler and more romatic times.

Although he lived to be 92-years old Samuel Hood never saw the mountain to which he lent his name, nor either fork of the river, nor the valley fragrant with spring nor the city where Simon Benson chose to build his remarkable hotel. Yet it seems entirely possible that the Englishman, who was a bit of an individualist himself, might well have approved of the entire scene. A definite if indefinable mystique charms the community, created from a history born not of violence but of English lords, fruit tree planters, mighty mountains, winemakers and an early Portland millionaire who loved the Gorge and cherished its traditions.

Columbia Gorge Hotel, 1921. *Prentiss photo courtesy Oregon Historical Society.*

43

Roadside & Other Attractions III

Interstate-84, Hood River to Mosier;
Scenic Highway to Rowena; Interstate-84,
Rowena to Memaloose State Park

This tour varies from the others in this series because it includes both freeway and Scenic Highway driving and because it starts by heading *east* on I-84 and concludes by heading *west* on the same freeway, as only westbound traffic can exit to Memaloose State Park.

Go east from Hood River to where the eastern section of the Scenic Highway begins. The exit road is clearly marked by a large sign. (Westbound travelers who wish to travel this route can exit from I-84 near the town of Rowena).

The 9-mile loop starts at Mosier, a town founded in the 1850s by J. H. Mosier, who was born in Maryland in 1821 and arrived in Oregon at the age of 32. He and his wife operated a stage station at this site for several years. Mosier, a cabinet maker of some skill, was known for his collection of wooden books, done so realistically that more than one person attempted to open them to read their contents.

The Scenic Highway passes through the village and climbs to a point far above, passing through orchards along the way and emerging from them onto an arid plateau where the Columbia is hid from view several times.

The road passes Rowena Dell, now being developed as a residential area. The dell is a canyon in the basalt extending from the river up to Rowena Crest. It was known, once, as Hog Canyon, but residents of The Dalles arranged to have the name changed. It is generally believed the name Rowena comes from H.S. Rowe, a railroad company official in the 1880s, although romanticists insist it was named for a young girl who lived in the vicinity.

Rowena Crest is part of Mayer State Park. A large parking lot is available for those who wish to while away some time absorbing the scenery or taking pictures of it. The view here is markedly different, although no less dramatic, than is the one from Crown Point.

Across from Rowena Crest viewpoint is a Nature Conservancy Tract named in honor of former Oregon Governor Tom McCall, who had a great love for the Gorge.

The descent from Rowena Crest is via the Rowena Loops, another series of graceful curves similar to the descent from Crown Point, and at the bottom the road connects with Interstate-84. Here, across on the north side of the freeway, the lower level of Mayer State Park offers boat ramps and be. ches, while a turn to the left on I-84 leads to Memaloose State Park a few miles to the west.

Memaloose comes from the Chinook word "memalust", which means "to die." A number of islands were called Memaloose in the Columbia River before the dams raised the water level to the point where they were inundated. The park is a deservedly popular overnight camping spot overlooking the one Memaloose Island that remains above water level. The land for the park was donated by Roy D. Chatfield, who at one time was manager of the Mosier Fruit Growers Association.

The Indians had a ritual process for taking care of their dead. Bodies were placed on the island in the river, wrapped in skins or blankets, frequently in a sitting position, and surrounded by the items that might be

The Rowena Loops. *Gifford photo courtesy Oregon Historical Society.*

needed in the spirit world — knives, bows, arrows. The bodies were sheltered by grave houses of pole and bark.

These "islands of the dead" were commented upon by many explorers, including Lewis and Clark, and they had been in existence beyond the memory of the oldest Indians. It is one of the saddest commentaries of the times that the sites were sometimes looted by white men who carried off skulls or entire skeletons which had been bleached by time, thus totally disregarding the religion and the feelings of the Indians.

From Memaloose State Park campground one sees a lone white marker on the island in mid-river, beneath which lies buried one Victor Trevitt, a white man. Trevitt was a pioneer printer, land developer and businessman in The Dalles who was representative to the state legistature in 1858 and a senator in 1868.

Trevitt moved to San Francisco in 1882 and died the following January. He had always considered the Indians to be his friends and one of his final requests was that he be buried with them on Memaloose Island. When he died his body was shipped by steamer to Portland and thence by chartered boat to Memaloose where it was interred in a brick sealed tomb beneath a white granite stone. Thus, temporarily, his wish was fulfilled.

But progress intrudes even upon the desires of deceased white men and when the waters rose behind Bonneville Dam the Indian dead were removed, leaving Trevitt's body alone on the island, where it remains to this day.

So much for final requests.

Indian Burial Grounds on Memaloose Island. *Photo courtesy Oregon Historical Society.*

46

Wasco

Wasco County was created by the territorial legislature in January, 1854. It was then the largest county in the United States, a vast area encompassing some 130,000 square miles, or more than one-third larger than the present state of Oregon. The county boundaries extended east to the Rocky Mountains, including part of Yellowstone and all of Sun Valley, Idaho. Gradually 17 other counties, as well as portions of 3 other states, were carved from it until the county area was reduced to less than 2,400 square miles.

Wasco is the Americanization of various spellings and pronunciations of the name of an Indian tribe which may have been Wascopum or Wiss-co-pam or any one of several similar words. The county is noted for its agriculture, especially for its orchards and wheat fields. But the focal point is The Dalles, county seat and largest city in the Columbia River Gorge.

If one considers the possibility that the first North American settlers arrived via that Asian land bridge and settled on the Columbia at the site of Celilo Falls, then the probability is that this is the most ancient and therefore the most historic spot on the continent. However, in terms of white history, it goes back less than 2 centuries. Regardless, in The Dalles the sense of history has remained strong and continues as one of the themes prevalent in the city today.

Different opinions exist regarding the derivation of the name. One assumption is that it comes from the French word for flagstone — *dalle* — which the French fur traders applied to the narrows where the river flowed over flat, basaltic rocks. The stretch of the river here included Big Eddy, on the western end and just east of that The Long Narrows (known also as Fivemile Rapids, The Dalles or The Great Dalles). Farther east was Tenmile Rapids and, of course, Celilo Falls.

Others say the early voyagers gave the area the name "Le Grande Dalle de la Columbia," which they interpret as "The Great Trough of the Columbia," but that translation is disputed. It has been known also as Wascopum (twice), as Fort Lee, The Landing of The Dalles, Fort Dalles, Dalles Landing, Dalles, and Dalles City.

The Hudson's Bay Company set up a trading post here in 1820. Nathaniel Wyeth brought the first covered wagon supply train to the area in 1834

47

and the Methodist missionairies came in 1838. The latter first coined the name Wascopum.

A company of volunteers arrived in 1847 and called the place Fort Lee, after their captain. When Nathan Olney established a sutlers' store to accomodate the soldiers he found a white settler by name of Joseph Lavendure had already staked out a land claim and fenced off a few acres.

In 1850 a regiment of Army Regulars from Fort Vancouver established a 10-square mile military reservation named Fort Dalles. Six years later Captain Thomas Jordan caused a stir when he came to this still primitive fort and began to spend the government's money freely to build ornate houses and to entertain in high style.

William R. Gibson was the first postmaster, in 1851, when the name Dalles was used, but 2 years later it was changed back to the earlier Wascopum before the name The Dalles surfaced. The city was incorporated in 1857.

Mail service began in 1851 as Justin Chenowith covered the route by sailboat and the steamboat *James P. Flint* made the first upriver voyage to "The Dalles Landing" the same year.

The place was visited by just about every explorer who made it as far west as the Oregon Territory. Lewis and Clark camped at a bluff overlooking the river to dry out their equipment. The area, known as Fort Rock, is now being restored as a park. David Thompson journeyed through here for the NorthWest Company. The ill-fated Marcus Whitman, accompanied by the Rev. H.H. Spaulding and their wives — the first white women to cross America — passed through in the 1830s and in 1843 Captain Fremont and Kit Carson stopped over on their way to California. Fremont's log of that trip was based on mileage from The Dalles.

The people of The Dalles, acutely aware of their historic past, have a passion for preservation. Still standing is The Original Courthouse, now located on West Second Street. It was built in 1858 and housed a sheriff's office and 3 jail cells on the first floor. At that time a courtroom, reached by an outside staircase, was upstairs. The latter is now used for a meeting room with an inside stairwell leading up to it.

The Surgeon's Quarters, all that remains of Fort Dalles after 2 fires, now is a museum featuring relics, pictures, tools and furniture, with a collection of old horse drawn vehicles on the grounds.

At the intersection of Twelfth and Court Streets is a 20-foot high stone pillar which has a cleft in the top to form a natural pulpit. Methodist missionairies preached to the Indians from this spot but it is now used for easter Sunrise services.

The Dalles locale was the little end of the funnel, the point which virtually all those easterners, westward bound, passed through on their way to the Willamette Valley or the Washington Territory. It was the end of the overland portion of the *Oregon Trail*, traversed all the way from Missouri by travelers who had endured incredible hardships en route.

Some figures and quotes.

".....10,000 arrived in Oregon that year, but since it was a bad cholera year it was estimated an equal number had died along the trail."

".....13,000 started, 10,000 arrived," is the entry for another year.

When the pioneers reached The Dalles they knew the journey was almost finished. The long, dusty trail, the violent prairie or mountain storms, the marauding Indians harassing the wagon trains, the piles of stones marking the graves of loved ones who had died along the trail — all this was behind them. Ahead was the great river and somewhere down it a place they could settle into and call home.

Still, The Dalles was not much of a city until the boom began in 1860 with the discovery of gold in eastern Oregon and Idaho. Then The Dalles became a jumping off spot for the gold fields. One sign of the new affluence was 25 saloons, which probably didn't set too well with the missionaires but certainly won approval of the miners who bought their supplies in the town.

In 1866 Congress appropriated money for the construction of a building to be used as a U.S. Mint, but the building was never used for that purpose.

Pulpit Rock. *Photo by Oral Bullard.*

Another boom occured in Wasco county in the early 1900s. It was centered in the town of Ortley, high atop Seven Mile Hill above Rowena, some 7 miles southeast of Mosier.

Ortley was once a thriving community but not much remains. Some pieces of concrete that may have been part of the foundation of an old hotel. An outbuilding weathered by wind, sun and time. And, buried somewhere nearby, the dreams that brought people here, confident they would find wealth and happiness in what was designed as a model community.

Ortley was a developers scheme, hatched by the Hood River Orchard and Land Company, made up primarily of Hood River and Portland real estate and insurance brokers. Some, at that time, deplored the development as "pie in the sky." Apple pie, that is, for the name of the town came from the Ortley apple, a variety that was planted on this hill in abundance and which caused a boom and bust reminiscent of the gold strikes, with all of the activity crowded into a few short years.

The difference being that there was never a strike of any kind at Ortley, although for a while there was high living and dazzling visions strung along the golden thread of promise. It was a classic case of people plunking down money to bet on the come that never came.

This irrational act was abetted by the developers who created the proper atmosphere by having 200 Greek and Italian laborers come in to clear the land of scrub oak and plant it with neat and appealing rows of apple trees. Master carpenters were imported to build a fine hotel, a company store, a post office and community center where dances were held for the prospective clients who, enticed by newspaper ads and brochures, were met at the train depot and brought up the winding road in Franklin or Cadillac automobiles. Once at Ortley the frenetic activity of clearing, planting and building made the adrenalin flow even faster.

The town was laid out in the European fashion, with 1-acre plots so all the houses were congregated, allowing the proposed citizenry to live in this tight, comfortable community and then go out to their nearby orchard and pick the apple crop that was to provide them with continuing wealth.

Caught up by the view, the altitude and the promise, the newcomers bought home sites so fast the builders could not keep up with them. But while they waited they did so in comparative luxury, living in walled tents equipped with antique furniture and with Oriental rugs on the floor, their meals served from a central cookhouse.

If, in the first few years, the apple trees seemed to be struggling in this environment the developers said not to worry, they were guaranteed to grow. But neither dreams nor guarantees can survive bankruptcy, which occurred in 1919.

Records reveal that the post office was established in 1911 with L.D. Firebaugh as the first postmaster. The names of those who gambled and

50

lost are mercifully omitted, but the word is that family fortunes and savings dissappeared in a brief time for the hilltop was not suited for growing apples or fruit of any kind. Wheat definitely, apples never.

The post office was discontinued on November 30, 1922. Most of the people and the apple trees were gone by then. Now only the traces of old buildings remain.

The city of The Dalles has great views and its own peculiar landmarks. A 6-foot tall rooster sits on the spire of St. Peter's Landmark Church. Take the Scenic Drive to Sorosis Park, well above downtown, for a look at Mount Adams. The park sits on part of the bottom of the ancient Lake Condon. The ground north of the park, sediment once 1,400 feet deep, was swept away in one of the great floods near the end of the Ice Age.

The roar of the cars and trucks that race along I-84 has replaced the sound of the water surging through and over the now buried rapids and Celilo Falls but it has not disturbed the aura of history which has hung over the community for all the centuries since the Indians first came and made it their home.

Photo courtesy Evelyn Hallyburton Johnson.

Roadside & Other Attractions IV

Interstate-84, The Dalles to Maryhill Park

Just east of The Dalles on I-84, The Dalles Dam, while not as much of a showplace as Bonneville, sometimes features a train ride through the dam and powerhouse.

Still slightly farther east a sign reads "Ancient Indian Fishing Grounds, Fulton Canyon, Next Right." This exit road is for both Deschutes Park and Celilo Park.

The frontage road, paralleling the freeway, crosses the Deschutes River in about 3 miles. The Deschutes, rising in the Cascade Range, is a well-known fishing stream and there is a large overnight campground on the

The Umatilla House Hotel was considered the finest west of Denver. First built by E. J. Dixon in 1857, it burned down in 1878. A 120 room version was re-built in 1879. The hotel, at East First and Union Streets in The Dalles, was the main meeting place in the city for almost half a century. It was torn down in 1929. *Photo courtesy Paul Weigelt.*

east bank with the summertime population consisting mostly of fishing devotees.

The name of the river comes from the French-Canadian fur trappers who called it Riviere aux Chutes, or River of the Falls, a definition which presumably referred not to any falls in that river but to those in the Columbia, downstream from where the Deschutes entered it.

Lewis and Clark, in 1805, called it Towornehiooks, an Indian name, but on their return trip the following year renamed it Clark's River. But, over the years, the French name prevailed, Americanized as Deschutes.

For weary travelers of the Oregon Trail it was one more river — the last — to cross before they reached The Dalles. Indians congregated here to watch as the prairie schooners were floated across. Livestock swam the river, but the Indians ferried women and children in their canoes, collecting trade goods for their labor.

If, instead of taking the frontage road at the I-84 exit, a left turn under the freeway leads to a rather pleasant park with the peaceful, impounded waters of the Columbia lapping gently at its far edges.

Sometimes, in the summer months, ice cream bars or snacks are for sale. Sea gulls meander on the broad lawn, racing to greet the tourist who tosses scraps of food to them. They seem, somehow, to be searching rather wistfully for the past when their ancestors could feast on the entrails of the salmon the Indians cleaned.

No one is certain from whence came the name Celilo or what it means. It may have been named after an Indian chief of after an Indian tribe. Some insist it means 'tumbling waters." The area has been known as Celilo since 1859, although the French called it The Chutes which was a name they used for all river falls. Early travelers knew it as a brutal portage and a wild ride through the "great whorl and suck" of the rapids.

The falls are buried beneath water behind The Dalles Dam so the name seems relatively unimportant. The history of the place lives on in old photographs and old memories. If the history is not known by the casual traveler it becomes just another pleasant place to stop and sit for awhile beneath the trees where the ever present wind stirs the leaves and sets them to sighing softly.

To complete this tour return to the freeway and head east to Biggs, then turn off on to Highway 97 and cross the Columbia via the Sam Hill Bridge. A right turn immediately after the crossing, and before going up the hill, leads to Maryhill State Park, equipped with modern restrooms and other facilities.

This is the first stop on the north shore. Well above Maryhill Park are two structures of interest to inspect when the next tour begins. But first the history of Klickitat County, perhaps the most boisterous of any county in the Gorge.

Klickitat

The Erastus Joslyn family, mentioned earlier, were probably the first permanent settlers, and for a short time following the Indian war the only settlers, in Klickitat County. So most of the county history begins after 1858, or when General Wool's order was rescinded.

The year 1859 is generally used as the time when this settlement began, with Amos Stark's homestead recorded in that year. One source claims Stark had spent 3 or 4 days in the vicinity of what was to become the town of Columbus in 1852 and filed a Mexican War Claim for much of the low land along the Columbia, but then headed for California and the gold fields, returning in 1859 to settle on his land.

However, there are other claims establishing county settlement in 1858, among them the Thorp and Splawn families. And there are 2 different dates given for the year John Golden arrived. His daughter, in an interview with the *Oregon Jounal's* Fred Lockley on January 5, 1925, is quoted as saying her parents moved to Klickitat on July 6, 1858, and further states that "there were only six white families in the county then." A version of Golden's biography claims he first arrived on July 9, 1859, with a herd of cattle.

Regardless of the exact date of his arrival, John Golden was one of the early settlers and certainly one of the outstanding characters and leaders in early Klickitat County history.

According to his published biography Golden was born in Westmoreland County, Pennsylvania, on March 18, 1826, and crossed the plains to California in 1852, which was the year when more than 10,000 persons were stricken by cholera as they moved westward.

Golden arrived in California in September of that year and spent some time mining on the American River, then moved to Shasta City where he remained until 1856.

Again, there are conflicts between his biography and his daughter's recollections, the latter claiming he came to Oregon directly from the east in 1853 and the following year moved to Yreka, California, before returning to Oregon a few years later to become partners with Louis Parrott in the cattle business.

In any event, sometime in the mid-1850s, Golden and a partner "took a contract to deliver one thousand four hundred hogs in California,

Klickitat County pioneer John Golden was a flamboyant entrepreneur who operated a number of sawmills and founded the town of Goldendale. A native of Pennsylvania, he migrated to California when he was 26 years old and moved to Klickitat when he was in his early 30s, taking with him his teenage bride Jane Gill Parrott. *Photo courtesy Klickitat County Historical Society.*

attempting to fulfill it by driving overland from Oregon. But heavy storms overtook them at Yreka, threatening to ruin them. They averted this calamity by turning most of the hogs into bacon, which they sold at an enormous profit."

On either May 17, 1858 or the same date, 1859 (depending on the source) Golden married Jane Parrott, his partner's daughter, who was at that time not quite 14 years old, and less than 2 months later moved with her to Klickitat County.

Golden operated sawmills at several locations, then in 1872 platted the town of Goldendale on land he purchased the previous year from L.L. Kimberland. On November 8 of that year an election was held to decide on the county seat. Goldendale received 77 votes, Rockland 78. It was estimated there were 500 persons living in the county at that time.

Six years later there was another election and this time Goldendale was selected as the county seat by a wide margin.

The early history of Klikitat County is the story of independent persons — sometimes upright and sometimes not — who chose to operate their county without interference from the Washington Territorial Government. Frontier justice was the rule.

From another Fred Lockley story which appeard in the *Oregon Jounal* on December 8, 1929, comes the tale of the fearful winter of 1862, 3 years after the county was formed, when it snowed continously from December 22 to January 1 and this was followed by a sleet storm which crusted the snow so badly that the jackrabbits and prairie chickens, unable to get their food supply through the ice crust, died in droves.

In the same article Lockley mentions that no town existed in the county then but there was a store at Columbus (then located approximately where Maryhill State Park is now). This store was purchased by a man who, despite the lack of a license to do so, began to sell liquor to the Indians, which riled the other settlers who no doubt remembered the recent Indian war and were against anything that could start another uprising.

Thomas Jenkins, whose family lived near the store, asked the salonkeeper to quit dispensing the booze, which only caused the man to become defiant and abusive. So Jenkins rounded up a party consisting of himself, Nelson Whitney, Louis Parrott, Stanton H. Jones and William Hicinbotham and the group marched on the saloon, grabbed and then discharged the loaded shotgun which the saloonkeeper kept on a wall in the store, and then began to systematically empty the whiskey out of the casks and destroy them. The saloonkeeper soon left in search of a friendlier atmosphere.

The few settlers opposed the idea of organized county government as it meant taxes would have to be levied and paid. So nobody stood for election to the county offices, causing the government at Olympia to appoint persons to them. The territorial government lacked the authority to compel these persons to take office so many of them refused to do so. Some

Canyon Road led from the old town of Columbus up to Maryhill. *Photo courtesy Oregon Historical Society.*

of those who did took full advantage of their position, as Fred Lockley related in the *Oregon Journal* in a story dated December 8, 1929: "Before the county was organized some of the officials appointed by the territorial legislature collected taxes from those who were willing to pay. The officials met, put all the taxes collected in a jackpot and divided them among themselves.

"In 1865 the sheriff collected from all who were willing to pay a tax, and left the county with all he had collected, leaving the other officers in the lurch, so the following year no attempt was made to collect taxes."

In 1867, after 8 years of county mismanagement or no management, a sheriff came from Olympia with a warrant from the Territorial District Court, charging the officials with failure to perform their duties.

The Sheriff took the lot of them to Snoqualamie where they were lodged overnight in a hotel — better accomodations than they had anticipated — and taken before the judge the next morning. The judge pointed to the flag in the courtroom and lectured the men on the Constitution of the United States and rights, privileges and obligations under it.

It must have been a pretty good speech for the records show that when the officials got back home they rented a building at Rockland, for $8 a month, used it as a courthouse and finally began to function, levying and collecting the first honest taxes in the history of Klickitat County.

Still another remarkable Klickitat character was a Methodist minister known as Father Wilbur.

James Henry Wilbur was born September 11, 1811, in New York State. In March, 1831, he married Lucretia Ann Stephens.

He was a giant of a man, standing six feet four and weighing almost 300 pounds which, it was said, was all brawn and muscle. He was a policeman in New York City for a time, but never carried a gun. Once, when 2 thugs attacked him, he seized each of them by the nape of the neck and banged their heads together with such force they both had to be hospitalized.

After becoming a minister Wilbur followed George Gray to the Oregon Mission in 1846, settling in Douglas County. He was instrumental in founding Umpqua Academy and other educational institutions and the town of Wilbur, Oregon, was named after him.

Wilbur made many trips up the Columbia River and was admired by the Indians around the Cascades who called him "Siwash Tyee" (Indian Boss). It is believed it was these Indians who first started calling him Father Wilbur.

At one point an Indian chief by the name of Skaminah became dissatisfied with some of the white settlers encroachments and began to stir up his tribe to perform hostile acts. Father Wilbur went with the sheriff to arrest him and when the chief resisted Father Wilbur reached out, seized him by the hair and started for Grand Dalles with the chief in tow. The chief did not want to board the boat to cross the river but became a true believer when Father Wilbur reached for his hair again.

Brought before the judge at The Dalles, with Father Wilbur standing by, the chief promised to keep the peace. A promise which he kept, as he did not allow his warriors to participate in the uprising of 1856.

Father Wilbur remained in the Northwest until his death in Walla Walla in October, 1887. Among his trademarks was that he rode a mule wherever he went, deeming that because of his size no horse was strong enough to support him adequately.

A compassionate man, Father Wilbur was disturbed when the military campaigns of Wright, Steptoe and Garnett crushed the Indians completely, and he got a cattleman named Ben Snipes to donate some of his cattle to the Indians so they could start their own herd.

Then, upset by the actions of the Indian agent, he went to the agent's office to protest and was ordered off the reservation. Despite the fact that it was wintertime, Father Wilbur took off for faraway Washington D.C., to confront President Lincoln with his version of the Indians plight. The president appointed Wilbur as Indian agent at Fort Simcoe, a post he held until 1882.

The town of Grand Dalles, from which point Father Wilbur crossed the Columbia with Chief Skaminah, was known by a number of names: Rockport, Grand Dalles, Rockland, North Dalles and, ultimately, Dallesport. It was also the site of another incident in Klickitat County history which reveals the tenor of the times.

Western promoters flourished and sometimes ran advertisements in Eastern newspapers which, to put it mildly, were gross exaggerations. Two men in the Grand Dalles prospered for awhile from their ads proclaiming investment opportunities available in that community.

Prospered, that is, until a lady who had invested in one of their schemes came west to check it out and discovered that no such business existed in this barren spot on the north shore of the Columbia.

In the true tradition of Klickitat County she went to a shop and purchased a blacksnake whip, entered the shysters office and flailed away at them, drove them into and down the street while the cowboys lining it cheered her on.

Except for Bingen and White Salmon, at the west end of the county, towns along the Columbia in Klickitat County had a difficult time of it. One of the earliest communities was the town of Columbus, which developed schools, stores, a church, postoffice and other amenities. There were orchards nearby and for awhile the town prospered.

Survival, however, became a problem with which it was unable to cope, due at least in part to the overpowering presence of the dominant force in eastern Klickitat County in the early Twentieth Century, Sam Hill.

In 1907 Hill became doggedly persistent in his attempts to buy the best land available. Harvey Lindley, a Quaker who had founded the city of Whittier, California, was said to have been Hill's agent in the land purchases and was largely responsible for the first 5,000 acres acquired. At one time the Hill holdings were divided into 40-acre tracts but the Quakers never flocked to the scene as Sam Hill had hoped they would and the small farm plan was later abandoned.

Hill put a railroad station in the town, causing relocation of the inhabitants in the process and, not being able to win over the populace of Columbus, planned a city of his own, Maryhill, on the benchland above it. He platted out 34 blocks, built the St. James Hotel and a land company office and garage, with houses for laborers behind it.

A small house on the land, known as Mary's Cottage, was sometimes used by Hill's daughter, Mary. After World War I the St. James Hotel became known as the Meadowlark Inn and was operated from 1931 to 1954 by 2 maiden ladies of English descent, Lucy Leatherby and Mary Carter, who had once served as cook and housekeeper for Sam Hill.

By 1922 the town of Columbus had surrendered to Hill's influence and the name of the post office was changed to Maryhill. Even so, the town that had struggled so hard to survive ended up dying a rather inglorius death.

During the 1930s some of Sam Hill's Maryhill buildings and also Mary's Cottage were torn down for salvage of lumber, the store burned at about the same time, the other buildings were vandalized and then vanished in one of the grass fires in 1958.

Monuments to a True Eccentric

It has often been noted that the stone Vista House on Crown Point, near the western end of the Columbia River Gorge, appears from a distance to bear a strong resemblance to an European castle. Thus, it seems appropriate that another castle should anchor the eastern end of the Gorge.

And indeed one does.

The Maryhill Museum, brainchild of Sam Hill, the entrepreneur, builder and dreamer who pushed so hard for the creation of the Scenic Highway along the south shore of the Gorge, sits on the arid benchland on the north shore above the Columbia more than 100 miles east of Vancouver. It is a lonely, although rather splendid, anachronism, and those who visit it for the first time are well advised to learn something of its history as well as the background of its founder, else they will find it a strange museum indeed. Even then, the museum will still seem somewhat apart from the ordinary.

As was Sam Hill.

His impact on the Gorge of the Columbia was greater than that of any other individual. For a span of at least 2 decades he was the dominant figure and, since he was a doer, he built monuments that remain.

Sam Hill was a giant of his age, with all of the marvelous eccentricities which only giants can truly afford to have. He was, basically, a self-made man who traveled in the fast lane of life in the early Twentieth Century, mingling with royalty, with visionairies, with persons of great wealth, befriending these but many others as well, including in at least one case a lady who had small talents but eccentricities to match his own.

Hill was born in North Carolina in 1857. His father, a physician, had strong Union sympathies and as the Civil War began moved his family to Minnesota. The father died when Sam was about 10 years old but the boy persevered, eventually graduated from Harvard Law School and became an attorney for James J. Hill, the railroad magnate (no relation) who had 7 daughters.

One, Mary, became Sam Hill's wife and they settled in Seattle. But he was not the type to remain in one spot permanently. He wandered a great deal. Trips to Europe were not uncommon. His mind churned out ideas and was receptive to ideas from others, and if sometime the practical ideas got mixed up with the outrageous ones, well, the fun was in waiting to see which turned out the best.

A notable flop was his planned project for the north shore, conceived because he was convinced there must be an "ideal place" between the rain zone west of the Cascade Range and the dry zone east of it. This place, Hill decided, must be found and on it he would conduct an agricultural experiment, including a Quaker colony.

He set out to acquire a 100-mile long strip when someone convinced him they had found the proper location, but ended up settling for a mere 7,000 acres. However, despite some outpouring of his energies into this project it, like some others in his life, never received his complete attention and this undoubtedly contributed to the failure of the original plan, which started about 1907.

By 1908 Hill, accompanied by the engineer, Samuel Lancaster, was off to Europe to study their roads, and plans for the Scenic Highway seem to have occupied much of his time until construction began 5 years later.

By 1914, the highway construction moving right along even as his proposed Quaker empire seemed to be collapsing, Hill decided to build an impressive residence on his land. A castle, really, although it was never a home and no one, including Hill, seems to be quite sure if he ever intended it for that purpose. He called the structure Maryhill, after either his wife or daughter, both of whom bore that name, but from all reports his wife disliked the place and never set foot in it. When someone asked him her reasons for shunning it, Sam Hill peered out at the desolate, windswept view, and blandly stated that she "preferred the peace and quiet of our Seattle home."

Over the years many persons asked Sam Hill why he had built Maryhill and he had a habit of replying with whatever answer first came to mind that day. Thus he told one person he wanted to have a fit place to entertain his friend, King Albert, of Belgium; another that it was designed as a fortress to keep an unspecified enemy from invading North America via the Columbia River; and still others that he had intended, all along, for it to be a place of residence — or maybe a museum.

There are those who insist that although Sam could be hard boiled, practical and shrewd, he was at heart a romantic who had become infatuated with the memory of the castles he had seen on the Rhine and wanted one of his very own on the Columbia.

And the museum, some say, was not his idea at all, but that of an emotional dancer and actress named Loie Fuller, who claimed to have been born in a Chicago bar and had been once a child temperance lecturer. Loie always had a flair for the dramatic and she grasped eagerly at opportunities, including the one to turn Sam Hill's castle into a museum.

Loie Fuller had been, in America, a less than first rate dancer, who made it to Europe with some help from Sam Hill and others, took her act to Paris and finally won fame at the Folies Bergere with her speciality,

Entrepreneur Sam Hill built his very own castle above the Columbia and got the Queen of Romania to dedicate it as the Maryhill Museum of Fine Arts. *This 1972 photo by Allan J. DeLay courtesy Oregon Historical Society.*

a dance featuring yards and yards of cloth which she swirled through a maze of colored lights. A publicist coined the name, Fairy of Light, for La Loie, as she became known, and she was a hit for a while.

A supercharged opportunist, she managed to parlay a rather ordinary skill, a few yards of cloth and some lights in the background, to friendships with the likes of Auguste Rodin, the sculptor, Isadora Duncan, of stage fame, and an entourage of what was termed "beautiful but demented ladies."

Shortly after the turn of the century, her sun in eclipse in Paris, Loie formed her own troupe of dancers but never again achieved the fame for which she hungered. So the years passed, her star plummeted, and then she learned her friend Sam Hill had this unfinished chateau on the bluff above the Columbia and heard opportunity knocking loudly at her door once again.

Loie offered to take charge of creating a museum which she would fill with French art, using her skill and Sam Hill's money. What evolved was the most dubious collection of "art" ever assembled — string collected by a Serbian queen, plaster casts of French medals and a collection of Rodin's works, the latter apparently to add a touch of authenticity to the entire collection.

Among Sam Hill's and Loie Fuller's mutual friends was Queen Marie of Romania. The queen herself was a bit of a character and not entirely foreign to opportunism. Born in England in 1875, daughter of the Duke of Edinburg and his wife, the Grand Duchess Marie, daughter of Czar Alexander II of Russian, this granddaughter of England's Queen Victoria became herself a queen when she married King Ferdinand of Romania.

Queen Marie and Sam Hill met in Russia in 1916 when she was visiting her mother's family and he was there because the American Railroad Association had sent him to advise the Russians on problems they were having on the Trans-Siberian Railway.

Eventually Sam, who collected honorary titles in abundance, was to become a member of the Queen's Body Guard of Romania, which wore well with his French Legion of Honor, his Commander of the Belgian Order of the Crown and the Order of the Sacred Treasures of Japan.

In 1926 someone came up with the idea of having Queen Marie come to America to dedicate Sam Hill's decaying castle with boarded up windows as a museum. It gave the queen a chance to tour America in style, at Sam's expense. A "good-will tour" it was termed. The less enchanted called it a publicity stunt engineered by Loie Fuller. And other skeptics said the queen was (1) in search of a rich American husband for her daughter, Ileana, who accompanied her on the trip, (2) seeking a loan from the United States for her country, or (3) hoping to sell some of her scripts to Hollywood.

She was, after all, a bit of a writer, having published magazine articles under the name Carmen Sylva as well as writing several books. She had already arranged to write a series of articles with titles such as "Why I Came to America," "My Impressions of America," and so on, and a total of 6 of these was produced, although the sharp-eyed noticed a known ghost writer in her entourage.

The trip got started with a royal flourish, a 21-gun salute on her arrival in New York. From that point on things went steadily downhill, although to give the queen her due she held up well under chaos. Maybe this was because of her training as an Army Nurse in World War I.

The trip arrangements had included that the Baltimore and Ohio Railroad would provide, free, a 10-car train for her party and the power to pull it when it ran over their tracks. Other railroad lines over which the train traveled were to furnish power for it on those occasions, but both the Southern Pacific and the Santa Fe balked at the idea. So, the queen never made it to California and Loie Fuller's possible dream of having a role in a Hollywood movie written by her royal friend didn't materialize.

Loie accompanied the queen on the trip, as did Alma de Bretteville Spreckels, another friend of royalty and wife of the sugar millionaire.

Not everyone welcomed the queen.

Labor leaders and war veterans in Canada protested because Romania owed their country 35 million dollars and hadn't yet got around to paying a cent of interest on the loan. The Ukranians squawked because they claimed Romania had mistreated European Ukranians, and New York Jews said the same for their compatriots in Romania. In Chicago a demonstration against the queen's visit had to be squelched and Cleveland was by-passed because a like disturbance was feared.

Through all this dissension Loie Fuller went her own way. She had her ballet troupe put on a benefit performance for the queen in New York, but it was alleged she pocketed all of the proceeds she could get her hands on.

There was intense competition among those who wanted to run the show. The B&O Railroad had appointed an Honorary Colonel, 73-year old John H. Carroll, as their official host and Carroll sided with the queen's special aide, Major Stanley Washburn, in resenting Sam Hill's intrusion into their own plans. Since the queen's designated reason for coming to America was "to dedicate Sam Hill's Maryhill Museum," and it was established he was paying a heavy part of her expenses, it got downright touchy as to who was in charge of what. And Loie Fuller, of course, was busy meddling in everyone's business and spreading tales, which eventually got her barred from the train.

It is said by those in attendance that on a cold November morning in 1926 Queen Marie of Romania gave one of her most memorable speeches as she dedicated her friend Sam Hill's museum on the bluff above the Columbia. But, as the reporters accompanying the train noted, when the queen viewed the desolation as she got off the train and saw the state of the building, she gave one quick look around and started to climb back on board. And rumor supplies the added story that she told Sam Hill at that point she was not going to participate in this farce, but then proceeded with the dedication when he pointedly reminded her who was paying for the trip.

During Queen Marie's "triumphal tour" across the land she had seen a rodeo, been "adopted" by the Sioux Indian tribe, and had met with the "common folk" she professed she wanted to know and become acquainted with in her search for the "real America."

But mostly it was royal shindigs of American nature. Of her appearance in Portland, author Stewart Holbrook wrote: "Lucky Portland, being only 114 miles from Maryhill and hence the city nearest to it, prepared for the event in Second Coming style."

But the backstage battles and maneuverings for position were beginning to show front and center. Alma Spreckels left the party in Portland when a blow-up occured because Sam Hill entered the queen's royal box at the Horse Show, causing both Colonel Carroll and Major Washburn to stomp out in a huff.

Regardless of the furor surrounding the event, Sam Hill's Museum was dedicated and when he died his will specified a Board of Trustees to look after it. Among the board members was Alma Spreckels, who gave, or loaned, many works of art to the museum. Meanwhile Clifford Dolph, the museum's first director, uncrated the collection amassed by Sam, with Loie Fuller's assistance, and between that and Alma Spreckel's generosity the empty rooms were filled and the museum opened in 1940. It sports an unlikely collection, considering its location; Russian icons, French paintings and sculpture, Indian artifacts, gilt furniture made for — and the museum claims partly by — Marie of Romania when she was Crown Princess — and a poster of Loie Fuller, the Fairy of Light.

At the time of Sam Hill's death there was no main road to the museum, the ultimate irony, considering his passion for good roads. For a time grass grew in the entrance ramps which he had designed to allow a car to drive up them and through the building, front to back.

So, traveler, enter this museum knowing it is one of two monuments created by a true eccentric, fired by a whim, possibly some old memory of a castle on the Rhine. A museum shaped not only by the personality of Sam Hill but also by his friends of natures both generous and erratic — a beautiful queen, an extremely wealthy American lady and a rather dumpy looking dancer who swathed herself in yards of cloth in her attempt to appear mysterious and romantic.

Just your everyday kind of sit-down to dinner group. At least to Sam Hill.

The second structure of Sam Hill's which remains in this locale is the Stonehenge replica that he built as a memorial to Klickitat County war

Loie Fuller created illusions by twirling yards of cloth through colored lights as she danced. This poster is on display at the museum. *Photo by Oral Bullard.*

dead and which was dedicated in July, 1918. It sits on land a short distance east of the Maryhill Museum and reflects his interest in Europe and European history.

The original Stonehenge is a prehistoric ritual monument in England. It dates back to the Bronze Age and is believed to have been built some time between 1300 and 1600, B.C. Considered structurally unique, it had appealed to Hill when he had seen it on the Salisbury Plains on one of his trips abroad.

He was, after all, a builder. It was he who built the Peace Arch, in Blaine, Washington, on the Canadian boarder, placing in it what he said was a small fragment from the Pilgrims ship, the Mayflower.

He chose to be buried on a rocky ledge below his Stonehenge replica, overlooking a scene he loved. He designed his own monument, but it was not built well enough to survive for long and it has since been replaced with another marker.

A plaque honoring Sam Hill was placed at Chanticleer Point, along the Scenic Highway, so his influence on the Gorge and its history is commemorated from one end to the other.

Sam Hill's Stonehenge was modeled after the English original. *Wesley Andrews photo courtesy Oregon Historical Society.*

Roadside & Other Attractions V

Washington State Highway 14, Maryhill to Bingen

In Konapee's time, and for many centuries prior to it, Indians congregated in the several mile long stretch of the Columbia above and below Celilo Falls. Evidence of their presence remains in petroglyphs and pictographs to be found in the stone cliffs near the railroad town of Wishram on the north shore across from Celilo Park, about 7 miles west of Maryhill.

Wishram was named for one of the Indian tribes which was known as either Wish Ham of Whiscom. The location was probably the most highly prized fishing spot the entire stretch of the Columbia and those who lived here in the old days were recognized as the elite.

Additional Indian drawings from an earlier time are located at Horsethief State Park, 3 miles west of Wishram. One of the most remarkable of these is a combination petroglyph (etched into stone) and pictograph (painted on stone) known as "She Who Watches You As You Go By."

Washington State Highway 14, proceeding west from Maryhill, runs along the rim above the Columbia River and thus affords a much different perspective than is gained from traveling along the water level route followed by the freeway on the opposite side of the river. Several turnouts enable the traveler to enjoy downstream views that can properly be described as spectacular, and a number of historical markers along the way give information regarding bygone days. One of these, above Horsethief Lake State Park, states that "salmon were smoked on racks over a heavy bed on coals and then packed in leaf lined baskets for winter use. Remains of underground 'pit houses' and many Indian artifacts have been discovered in this area by archaeologists. The Lewis and Clark expedition found several hundred Indians fishing here in 1805, as they had done for centuries."

The people who inhabited the Gorge prior to the coming of the white race had a complex civilization complete with their own legends, their own mores and code of ethics. We are all poorer for the eradication of that civilization. But how might it have been, such a short time ago, to stand on the bluff and look down at the busy carnival, to see the fish drying on racks along the bank or being smoked over the coals, to see horse racing, gambling, the bartering that went on, with probably some bickering and fighting thrown in for good measure.

One thing is certain; for a distance of more than 20 miles very little has changed on the land above the north shore of the Columbia, except for the view. Developers threaten to intrude, but at this writing have not yet succeeded. Summer campers crowd into Horsethief Lake State Park, one of the better parks in the Gorge. East of the town of Lyle there are some remarkable symmetrical pillars known as the Paha cliffs. According to legend, Speelyei, the coyote god, turned mortals into stone to create these formations.

Lyle is 23 miles west of Maryhill and it is here the Klickitat River meets with the Columbia. The town was first known as Klickitat Landing but when James O. Lyle purchased the site from J.W. Williamson and platted the town the post office took his name and thus it has remained ever since.

One mile west of Lyle is a lovely rest area which offers superb views both up and downriver, including one of Memaloose Island.

West of the rest area the highway descends to near river level again as it nears Bingen, directly across the Columbia from Hood River.

Bingen was founded in 1892 by P.J. Suksdorf and the name comes from the European Bingen-on-the-Rhine because the founder saw some simi-

Photo courtesy Oregon Historical Society.

70

larity between the position on the Columbia and the German town's location on the Rhine.

Bingen is the home of Bingen Wine Cellars. The winery is located in the heart of town and is open for wine tasting Thursday through Saturday afternoons. The building it occupies is a former apple and pear warehouse whose thick walls make it easy for the temperature control necessary for winemaking. The grapes, first planted in 1964, come from the Mont Elise Vineyards which are on a southern slope overlooking the Columbia River Gorge.

Both Bingen and its sister city, White Salmon, which adjoins it immediately above on Highway 141, have been refurbished to reflect Bingen's European namesake. The name White Salmon is from the great numbers of salmon which abounded in the river each fall and which turned white during the spawning run. This town site was at one time purchased by a supply of bacon and potatoes, but today it is a thriving community overlooking the Gorge.

Photo courtesy Oregon Historical Society.

Roadside & Other Attractions VI

Klickitat River Loop

Although the Washington Territorial Legislature spelled the county name with a C, i.e., Clickitat, when it was established in 1859, that same year the surveyor-general of the territory applied the current spelling, Klickitat, to the river which rises from a glacier on Mount Adams. Over the years the river spelling won out and was adopted for the county and eventually the town of the same name.

Two meanings are listed for the name; "robber" and "beyond." The latter is generally believed to be the definition used by most of the Indians which resided in this area between the coastal-river tribes and those east of the Cascade Range.

A portion of this tour parallels the beautiful Klickitat River through country that offers a great variety of views including a close-up of mighty Mount Adams and the relatively unspoiled country near its base.

Start at the west edge of the town of Lyle on Highway 142, along the east side of the river. The first 2 miles the road runs above the steep canyon then descends gradually for the next 2 miles until it is at almost water level, where it remains for the next 15 miles. The road crosses the river 3 times, at miles 10, 17 and 19, and for much of this distance it is virtually at streamside. The town of Klickitat, originally named Wrights after early settler L.C. Wright but renamed in 1910, is a lumbering community 13 miles from Highway 14.

After the last river crossing the road begins a 4-mile long, twisting climb, with turnouts offering views down into the valley. Then, abruptly, the road levels out at the top and Mount Adams looms ahead to the left. A mile after that a road to the left leads to Glenwood.

Take the road toward Glenwood and after a short drive begin to be treated to some marvelous views of the valley of the Klickitat, into which the road begins to descend after 6 miles via a long, winding route known as the Glenwood Grade. After 5 miles it reaches a bridge across the Klickitat and then the climb begins again, this time with the river on the right and the valley not visible from the road. However, 6 miles from the bridge, exit at a viewpoint sign and follow the dirt road three-tenths of a mile to a turnaround from which a few step walk to a fence offers a variety of scenic glimpses into the valley.

As you emerge from the viwpoint road Mount Adams appears at the end

Klickitat River valley from viewpoint. *Photo by Oral Bullard*

Outlet Falls. *Photo by Oral Bullard*

of the highway. Exactly eight-tenths of a mile later keep an eye out for a small brown wooden sign tacked onto a tree on the right hand side of the road. The lettering on it is nearly illegible but the words "Outlet Falls" can be made out. Pull off the road and park. *Handhold children and put pets on a leash.* A very short walk leads to a precipice overlooking the pool below Outlet Falls, where the stream (a feeder to the Klickitat River) rushes through a narrow chasm in the rocks to the left and plunges over a cliff to form the pool. Particularly early in the season, when the water is draining rapidly from the meadows above, this is a truly spectacular sight to look down on. But do take precautions with small children and pets at this point, and be careful yourself.

A short distance past Outlet Falls the road emerges from the woods into open meadows with the stream swirling through them. The scene here becomes very bucolic. A number of return routes to Highway 14 are available but the one recommended is to continue on to Glenwood (so named because it is in a small valley surrounded by forests) and turn south on Highway 141, with which the road intersects at the east side of Trout Lake.

A visit to the community of Trout Lake (named for the nearby lake) will prove interesting, but a left turn on 141 will lead back to the town of White Salmon, then down to Bingen and Highway 14 along the Columbia River.

Skamania

Skamania County is a paradise for campers, hikers and all who love the outdoors. Many Forest Service campgrounds and miles and miles of trails are available.

Before delving into the county's history it seems appropriate to remark that the area was recognized by the Indians to be as enjoyable as the white race later found it to be. A large section of the county is known today as Indian Heaven and portions of the huckleberry fields are set aside for picking by Indians only.

The adventurous can take trails into Indian Heaven, can climb Red Mountain from which they can view the Indian Race Track, with the indentation in the land still visible, can tour along dozens of streams to literally hundreds of lakes. (At the back of this book a number of books are noted which list trails and other enticements in the area. Please do not venture into the back country without adequate equipment and guide books or U.S.G.S maps which delineate the routes to be followed.)

Since virtually the entire back country is along U.S. Forest Service roads we do not list a trip into it as one of our regular tours. However, for those who wish to explore a bit take either of the 2 exits from Highway 14 to the town of Carson. A sign on road 30 soon indicates Mount St. Helens Viewpoint, 28 miles, and that is true. However, be advised this viewpoint is from the east side of the mountain, which is seen only from a distance. An interesting view — or views, as there are several along the route but not the more sensational one available from the north side of the mountain. A few picnic tables sitting in the open and a pit toilet are the only amenities at the designated viewpoint.

Shortly after this a sign at an intersection indicates Sawtooth Berry Fields, 8 and Trout Lake, 29 miles. If you follow this route you will sometimes be on a gravel road; on a clear day you will get a brief glimpse of Mount Rainier; and you will get several clear views of Mount Adams. If you continue on far enough, a few miles past the berry fields, you will come to a large wooden sign which contains a map of the Mount Adams recreation Area. The altitude here is 4,000 feet, the view of Mount Adams is breathtaking.

The roads are well signed and there are innumerable ways to get back to Carson or the communities of Willard (named for an early day rancher

Mount Adams from viewpoint in Gifford Pinchot National Forest. *Photo by Oral Bullard.*

and county commissioner) or Underwood (named for Amos Underwood, who settled here in 1875) or Cook (which was initially a steamboat landing on the Columbia, named for Charles A. Cook, who homesteaded the site), about 10 miles east of the Carson exit from Highway 14.

A few special notes about driving in the back country. (1) The roads may be either hard surfaced or gravel. Frequently there is a little if any warning when the hard surfacing ends. Control you speed (I keep mine around 30 mph) on gravel roads, for they can be tricky for a driver not used to them. (2) In logging country (which this is) logging trucks *always* have the right of way. *Believe it*!!! (3) The entire road system in the high country will be open only from mid-July to late October. Remember this and avoid taking it too early in the year — as I did and ended up stuck in a snow bank in mid-June. (4) During the hunting season don't get out of your vehicle and go crashing around in the underbrush. *Do* wear bright clothes but stay in the car, close to the car, or in the open if possible.

Finally, the fall colors are truly impressive, it's my favorite time to visit Indian Heaven.

Skamania County was organized in 1854 with its western boundary at the southwest corner the cliffs of Cape Horn on the Columbia and the eastern county line the Rocky Mountains. So, in respect to size at least, it was a sister to Wasco County.

Skamania is an Indian word meaning "swift waters" and refers, in this context, to the Columbia River. (The hamlet of Skamania, along the Columbia, was for many years known as Butler, but the citizens petitioned to have it changed to the county name).

Skamania County is rich in both Indian lore and early white history. The legendary Bridge of the Gods extended from the north to the south shore at the location of the modern bridge by the same name. There is a controversy about how the Cascade Rapids in the Columbia were created. Historical signs in the area claim that more than 800 years ago part of a mountain 4 miles to the northwest slid into the river and dammed it, and cites as proof the remains of Indian villages found buried in the locale. Indian legends claim there was once a stone arch spanning the river and the rapids were created when it collapsed.

It was at this point, the site of the Upper Cascades, that the Indians launched their attack on March 26, 1856, when they felt threatened by the ever increasing number of whites. Just west of here Captain H.D. Wallen and Lieutenant H.D. Hodes, along with soldiers of the U.S. Army, had built a blockhouse the previous November. They named it Fort Rains, for Major Gabriel Rains, and installed a mounted howitzer to provide protection for military cargo on the portage road from the upper landing to the boat landing 3 miles downstream. When the attack came, Sergeant Matthew Kelly and 8 soldiers, firing through the gun holes of the overhanging second story,

Middle Blockhouse, built in 1855 at the Cascades on the north shore of the Columbia. *Photo courtesy Oregon Historical Society.*

successfully defended the fort for 3 days, although 2 soldiers and several settlers were killed.

The siege was lifted when Colonel E. J. Steptoe and a detachment of regulars arrived from the Dalles and Lieutenant Phil Sheridan and a company of dragoons moved upriver from Fort Vancouver. This particular location is still known as Sheridan's Point.

The Wind River country was settled beginning in the 1870s and in the 1880s a sawmill was started by a man named Borthwick at the present site of the town of Carson. Also in the 1880s another settler by the name of Casner came to live at the mouth of the creek.

About 1895 a store and post office were established here and the petitioner for the latter decided to honor Casner, the early settler, by naming it after him. Unfortunately, the petitioner's handwriting was so poor that whoever read the application decided it was meant to be "Carson" and so that name was applied to the town.

Like other communities on the north shore, Carson boomed when the railroad was built. Several sawmills were situated in the town and in 1905 and for several years thereafter as construction of the railroad progressed Carson was one of the liveliest spots around, boasting "nine saloons and dance halls with all the girls and trimmings."

The town is the gateway to the Wind River country and is also known as the home of St. Martin's Hot Springs, located on the west bank of the Wind River a short distance north of Highway 14.

The presence of hot springs in Skamania County is a fairly common occurrence. The Collins Hot Springs Hotel was established just east of the town of Stevenson in the early 1900s. Charles T. Belcher secured a 15-year lease on the property and started a bath house with porcelain tubs — because the mineral content of the water prohibited the use of the more widely used metal tubs.

Collins Hot Springs was quite close to the Columbia and had been submerged several times by high water so a concrete flue was built to protect them from future damage of this nature and Belcher also added a 96-room, 3-story hotel.

Many persons came from Portland by river boat to enjoy what they believed to be the medicinal value of the hot springs water. When the railroad was built along the north shore a hospital was established here during the construction years. Later, after the railroad had been finished along the south shore, the hotel furnished launch service across the Columbia to transport Portland passengers to it.

For a decade and a half this remained a popular spot, then Belcher sold the hotel, business fell off and the community gradually faded from view. The hotel finally was torn down.

Another hot springs hotel no longer in existence was one developed at Government Soda Springs. This, like the hotel at Collins, was well known

Wesley Andrews photo courtesy Oregon Historical Society.

for a number of years but it had a short operating season because of the climate and its comparative remoteness, so it was difficult to make it profitable. The hotel burned down in 1937.

Still a third hotel, known as Shipherd's Springs, was located north of St. Martin's hotel and was also popular for awhile. However it was not rebuilt after it burned down.

No such fate befell St. Martin's Hot Springs Hotel, which remains in operation to this day. The springs were discovered by Isadore St. Martin after he moved from the village of Cook in 1870. When he went deer hunting that winter with a friend they noticed steam rising from a spot on the west side of Wind River, discovered the springs but decided to keep them a secret.

Then, in 1881, when Mrs. Martin was suffering severely from neuralgia, her husband took her to bathe in the springs and later built a shelter there. Hot springs being very big in those days the fame of St. Martin's spread rapidly and people came to camp out in tents nearby. The resort hotel was built in 1899 and the present bath house established in 1923.

Isadore St. Martin was no longer around by then. In 1910 he was stabbed to death by a man named Brown who had made disparaging remarks about the quality of the water. St. Martin ordered him off the land, an argument ensued, and St. Martin was killed.

The hotel is opened to the public year around and the baths are still enjoyed by many.

Another Skamania County landmark is Beacon Rock. It can be seen easily from Crown Point and for many miles along I-84 it looms as the dominant water level feature on the north shore.

The 800-foot high volcanic plug was sturdy enough to resist the many floods and was thus exposed from the subterranean position it occupied originally.

The first recorded owner of the rock was a pioneer named Phillip Ritz, who sold it in 1870 to Jay Cooke, an Eastern financier who later was involved in a gigantic scandal. What created Cooke's interest in the rock has never been made public. From Cooke, ownership passed to Charles Ladd of Portland, in 1904, then to Henry J. Biddle.

Biddle published a book about the rock, titled "Beacon Rock on the Columbia, Legends and Traditions of a Famous Landmark." In the book he stated: "Mr. Ladd's idea was always to preserve the rock from defacement, and when he and his associates sold it to me a clause was inserted in the deed to that effect. My purpose in acquiring the property was simply and wholly that I might build a trail to the summit...."

Biddle comments several times on the Indian superstitions regarding the rock but appeared unfamiliar with the legend of Whehatpolitan (also known as Che-che-optin), an Indian princess who climbed to the top of

Boating scene, about 1900, near Beacon Rock. *Photo courtesy Oregon Historical Society.*

the rock with her baby to escape from her angry father. She was unable to get back down, the baby perished, and legend says the wails of mother and child can still be heard at certain times.

Just how Whehatpolitan managed to get to the top of the 17-acre rock is not known. No white man climbed it until Frank Smith and 2 others scaled the monolith in 1901. Prior to that the only known climbers were Turner Leavens goats who were occasionally seen at the summit.

From Biddle's book: "Work was commenced on the trail in October, 1915, and it was completed in April, 1918. Omitting the time lost in the winter, about two years were consumed in the work . . . I was fortunate at the start in securing a very competent foreman in the person of Charles Johnson, who held a similar position in the building of the Columbia River Highway . . .

"Owing to the steepness of the rock it was impossible to survey much of it in advance, all that could be done was to drive a narrow trail ahead, selecting the most suitable points as they were reached."

The "competent foreman" Biddle mentioned, Charles Johnson, was known also as "Tin Can Johnson." He and Biddle worked on the trail construction together and Johnson used 2 sure-footed burros, deeming this the best method to carry tools, cement and gravel up the side as required.

The trail, when completed, was 4,500 feet long. It still provides an interesting and rather easy walk to the top for thousands of persons yearly. The trail was built for a cost of approximately $10,000, and gains about a foot in altitude every 5 feet walked.

All of this time, effort, money and dreams threatened to be for naught in 1931 when the U.S. Army Corps of Engineers, never willing to let a good rock go to waste as mere scenery, decided it would make a nice jetty at the mouth of the Columbia and made plans to blow it up and barge it downriver. Biddle had passed on and his heirs had offered the rock to the state of Washington as a gift but a legal opinion was rendered that this constituted tax evasion, so the gift offer was rejected.

Hearing of the Corps plans and wanting to preserve the landmark, Sam Boardman, the Parks Engineer for the Oregon State Parks Commission, puckishly suggested that Oregon accept the gift of the rock and establish an Oregon State Park in the State of Washington. This created such a furor that Washington State finally created Beacon Rock State Park, so the famous rock was saved for future generations to admire and enjoy.

Beacon Rock State campground is across Highway 14 from the rock and has modern overnight camping facilities, plus a short and interesting hike of about 1 mile to Rodney Falls - Hardy Falls. The trailhead is in the park itself and it is mostly level walking from there to Rodney Falls where the cataract plunges into a pool, then rushes out through a narrow slit to continue its drop as Hardy Falls.

This is part of the Hamilton Mountain Trail, which continues on for another 3 miles to the top of the mountain. It is quite steep, with 72

84

switchbacks. Definitely not for the weary legged but worth a bit of effort to get far enough up it to take in the view.

The town of Stevenson, located on Highway 14, is the Skamania county seat, an honor first held by the Lower Cascades. But the location was changed one dark night when the county commissioners, incensed because the rent had been increased on the building they were using, removed the county records and transferred them to Stevenson. The town was platted in 1894 by George H. Stevenson, who had come west from Missouri in 1880.

Boat rides on the Columbia Gorge Sternwheeler are available here. The museum is interesting, the library excellent, and there are some marvelous doughtnuts at a shop on the main street through town.

Roadside & Other Attractions VII

Highway 14, Bingen to Cape Horn

The Little White Salmon River forms the line between Klickitat and Skamania counties and for the west bound traveler it also signals a dramatic change in the mood along the river. Now to the west the cliffs become higher, the forest denser. In the winter the clouds hang low and fog shrouds the heights. One can sense the early explorers exhilaration as they reached this point. It was as if they could smell the ocean — journey's end.

The Columbia River Gorge Hotel sits directly across the river while above Highway 14 on the north shore is the Broughton Flume, in use for more than half a century.

The trough was built in the 1920s, using Douglas fir in 16-foot sections. It is 9 miles long and utilizes water from a dam on the Little White Salmon to carry the logs to the railroad 1,000 feet below the flume's starting point. A crew patrols the entire length of the chute on a walkway 12 inches wide. Flume damage, obstructions or excess water spillage is reported by an electronic warning system. The flume capacity is between 40 and 50 million board feet of lumber per year.

The community of Home Valley, founded about the year 1890, is located between Bingen and Stevenson. The founders were Scandanavian families who had come from the midwest to Cascade Locks and then crossed the Columbia to Skamania County because they were attracted by the free land available if they homesteaded. They decided the east side of the Wind River had climate and geographical features similar to their homeland, hence the name, Home Valley.

Kanaka Creek, east of Stevenson, is so named because the Hudsons Bay Comapny, in those days when it was a major force along the Columbia, brought a group over from the Sandwich (Hawaiian) Islands. The ship that bore them to the river was wrecked so the islanders remained, settling on this creek where the men married the Indian women. Eventually they moved to the reservation with their wives and families.

The town of North Bonneville, founded in 1932 when construction was scheuled to start on Bonneville Dam, has been completely rebuilt and relocated because of the second powerhouse at the dam. Construction on this powerhouse was begun in 1974 and completed in 1982. It features the usual tourist information services and a view down into the powerhouse itself as well as exhibits showing how power is produced.

Now the highway approaches the western end of the Gorge. As it was for the westbound travelers of old, this tour is nearing its end. Beacon Rock invites a visit, beyond it is the hamlet of Skamania and then the road begins to climb as it nears Cape Horn. That name was coined when the early river travelers met with rough water around the rocky promontory and they were reminded of rounding the Horn on the southern tip of South America.

The highway hugs the cliff high above the river and a turnout offers an opportunity for taking pictures of the marvelous upriver view.

Then Milepost 22 marks the end of Skamania County and is directly across the river from Crown Point.

Pioneer John W. Stevenson came west in 1853. This picture was taken at Cape Horn when he was 88 years old. *Photo courtesy Oregon Historical Society.*

Cape Horn is near western end of the Gorge. *This Lily E. White photo, taken in 1902, courtesy Oregon Historical Society.*

The Last Stop

Three miles into Clark County, at Milepost 19 on Highway 14, is a roadside sign which marks the last stop for the west-bound traveler following this tour of the Gorge along the North shore. The sign reads:

FIRST EXPLORERS
1792
South of here on what is now Reed Island, a party of British seamen, led by Lieutenant Wm. R. Broughton, claimed the Columbia River for Great Britain and named Mount Hood for a Lord of the Admiralty. They were from the crew of H.M.S. Chatham, the armed tender that accompanied Captain Vancouver's H.M.S. Discovery on its historic voyage to the New World, and were the first white men to explore the river above its mouth. After planting a British flag, all hands including a friendly Indian chief, joined in a toast to King George III. This claim to the river was relinquished in the U.S. - Canadian boundary treaty of 1846.

That was October. According to some of the old journals Lieutenant Broughton had, either earlier that day or the day previous, gone ashore near where the Washougal River joined the Columbia and met an old, red haired Indian chief by the name of Soto. These reports list Soto as the son of a Spanish mariner who had been shipwrecked on the Oregon coast about the year 1725. Captured by the Indians, the Spaniard stole a canoe, escaped his captors by paddling upstream where he met, fell in love with and married a beautiful Chinook maiden.

It is said that Konapee, the Spaniard, lived near Celilo Falls for several decades, during which he noticed that the Indians who came from the mountains and the plains each year brought with them more and more trade goods which he recognized as being of European origin.

Konapee reasoned there must be a route to the eastern coast and one day, before age debilitated him, he arose and departed from his Eden. He followed the Indian trails eastward until he arrived at Fort Mackinac, where he met Captain Rogers and told him of this mighty stream, the river Oregon, which drained the northwestern part of the continent and emptied into the western sea.

Thereafter the figure of Konapee fades into oblivion, to become only a faint shadow among the many shadows on the pages of Columbia River history. He is a part of the mystery and the myths that remain, as haunting as Whehatpolitan's wails from the top of Beacon Rock when the wind blows at midnight; as mystical as a hike up the Eagle Creek Canyon on a day when the ragged shreds of white fog hang in the branches along the trail.

In the days since Konapee's time millions of persons have traveled through the Gorge. A few have stayed but most, even today, follow the pioneers lead and pass on through. It remains beautiful, sparsely populated and subject to the whims of special interest groups who argue bitterly about how it may be used or preserved.

Despite the bridges, roads, railroads and dams there remain those constant reminders from the past. Among these is Tsa-gig-la-lal, known as She Who Watches You As You Go By, and she stares enigmatically across the silent water behind The Dalles Dam.

Since she is of indeterminate age she may have been there even before Konapee arrived, to be followed by other white men of various nationalities from all over the world. Despite their disparate backgrounds these men had one thing in common, they were not content to live with the river as Nature had created it and so they instituted the process of change which still goes on.

So Tsa-gig-la-lal watches, perhaps listening in vain for the 10,000 year roar from the rapids and falls which the new settlers have stilled, or perhaps only contemplating the future and wondering what changes or catastrophies it may bring to Konapee's Eden.

Acknowledgements

Every writer of history or legend builds on what others have written in earlier times. In the main, these writings are preserved in libraries and historical societies. Thus, I am extremely grateful both to those writers who recorded, and to those institutions on both sides of the Columbia River Gorge who preserved, these records.

The writing of *Konapee's Eden* was not a specific research project, but rather the result of several years random accumulation of facts, fantasies and fables — some passed on to me by word of mouth, others recorded on browned with age newsprint, tucked away in obscure files, or in old books drawn from the depths of a library, or sometimes from books still in circulation.

If I had had the foresight to make notes for a bibliography, that bibliography would extend for several pages. Failing to take those notes, I have listed, where direct quotes are used, the source of these quotes, both by writer and publication. And I list herewith other books still in circulation which I found interesting and informative and which I recommend wholeheartedly as additional reading on the subject of the Columbia Gorge and its history, as well as ways to explore it in greater depth.

Attwell, Jim, *Columbia River Gorge History* (Volume One), Tahlkie Books, 1974

Attwell, Jim, *Columbia River Gorge History* (Volume Two), Tahlkie Books, 1975

Hansen, Mel, *Indian Heaven Back Country,* The Touchstone Press, 1977

Lowe, Don & Roberta, *35 Hiking Trails, The Columbia River Gorge,* The Touchstone Press, 1980

McArthur, Lewis L., *Oregon Geographic Names,* (Fourth Edition), The Oregon Historical Society, 1974

Phillips, James W., *Washington State Place Names,* University of Washington Press, 1971

In thinking back to where the idea for the book was first formed I believe it was when I heard the story of four French sailors who were shipwrecked on the Oregon Coast in the mid-Eighteenth Century. Fearful of the Spaniards who they knew ruled California, they hiked south and east, in the general direction of New Orleans and, according to the teller of this tale, at least one of them survived the journey.

I can recall neither the teller nor the year in which the tale was told to me, but it was more than a decade ago. In the intervening years I heard other stories, and as I began to get serious about writing the book many persons volunteered tales that had been passed on to them, frequently through generations of their own family.

To all of these persons I am also grateful. Because of all the sources, named and unnamed, the history and the legends of the Columbia River Gorge came alive for me, and I am happy to share them with you.

Oral Bullard
Beaverton, Oregon
1985

Cover photo (used also on page 91)
"She Who Watches", by Don Lowe